Doggin'
The Carolina Coasts

The 50 Best Places
To Hike With Your Dog Along
The North Carolina and
South Carolina Shores

DOUG GELBERT

illustrations by

ANDREW CHESWORTH

Cruden Bay Books

There is always a new trail to look forward to...

DOGGIN' THE CAROLINA COASTS: THE 50 BEST PLACES
TO HIKE WITH YOUR DOG ALONG THE NORTH
CAROLINA AND SOUTH CAROLINA SHORES

Cruden Bay Books
PO Box 467
Montchanin, DE 19710
www.hikewithyourdog.com

International Standard Book Number 978-0-9795577-0-5

*"Dogs are our link to paradise...to sit with a dog on a hillside
on a glorious afternoon is to be back in Eden,
where doing nothing was not boring - it was peace."*
- Milan Kundera

Ahead On The Trail

No Dogs!   14

Ten Cool Things To See On The Trail With Your Dog   15

The 50 Best Places To Hike With Your Dog   19

Camping With Your Dog   107

Your Dog At The Beach   117

Doggin' The Chesapeake Bay   105

Index To Parks And Open Space   107

Also...

Hiking With Your Dog   5

Outfitting Your Dog For A Hike   9

Low Impact Hiking With Your Dog   12

Introduction

The Carolina coasts can be a great place to hike with your dog. Paw-friendly sand trails, shady maritime forests, some of the most historic grounds in the South, the estates of America's wealthiest families and some of the country's dog-friendliest beaches all beckon to your canine adventurer.

I have selected what I consider to be the 50 best places to take your dog for an outing on the Carolina coasts and ranked them according to subjective criteria including the variety of hikes available, opportunities for canine   swimming and pleasure of the walks. The rankings include a mix of parks that feature long walks and parks that contain short walks. Did I miss your favorite? Let us know at *www.hikewithyourdog. com*.

I have defined the Carolina coasts roughly to be those areas east of US Highway 17. For quick reference the titles of North Carolina parks are in black, South Carolina parks in gray.

For dog owners it is important to realize that not all parks are open to our best trail companions (see page 14 for a list of parks that do not allow dogs). It is sometimes hard to believe but not everyone loves dogs. We are, in fact, in the minority when compared with our non-dog owning neighbors.

So when visiting a park always keep your dog under control and clean up any messes and we can all expect our great parks to remain open to our dogs. And maybe some others will see the light as well. *Remember, every time you go out with your dog you are an ambassador for all dog owners.*

Grab that leash and hit the trail!
DBG

Hiking With Your Dog

So you want to start hiking with your dog. Hiking with your dog can be a fascinating way to explore the Carolina coasts from a canine perspective. Some things to consider:

🐾 Dog's Health

Hiking can be a wonderful preventative for any number of physical and behavioral disorders. One in every three dogs is overweight and running up trails and leaping through streams is great exercise to help keep pounds off. Hiking can also relieve boredom in a dog's routine and calm dogs prone to destructive habits. And hiking with your dog strengthens the overall owner/dog bond.

🐾 Breed of Dog

All dogs enjoy the new scents and sights of a trail. But some dogs are better suited to hiking than others. If you don't as yet have a hiking companion, select a breed that matches your interests. Do you look forward to an entire afternoon's hiking? You'll need a dog bred to keep up with such a pace, such as a retriever or a spaniel. Is a half-hour enough walking for you? It may not be for an energetic dog like a border collie. If you already have a hiking friend, tailor your plans to his abilities.

🐾 Conditioning

Just like humans, dogs need to be acclimated to the task at hand. An inactive dog cannot be expected to bounce from the easy chair in the den to complete a 3-hour hike. You must also be physically able to restrain your dog if confronted with distractions on the trail (like a scampering squirrel or a pack of joggers). Have your dog checked by a veterinarian before significantly increasing his activity level.

🐾 Weather

Hot humid summers do not do dogs any favors. With no sweat glands and only panting available to disperse body heat, dogs are much more susceptible to heat stroke than we are. Unusually rapid panting and/or a bright red tongue are signs of heat exhaustion in your pet.

Always carry enough water for your hike. Even days that don't seem too warm can cause discomfort in dark-coated dogs if the sun is shining brightly. In cold weather, short-coated breeds may require additional attention.

🐾 Trail Hazards

Dogs won't get poison ivy but they can transfer it to you. Some trails are littered with small pieces of broken glass that can slice a dog's paws. Nasty thorns can also blanket trails that we in shoes may never notice. At the beach beware of sand spurs that can often be present in scrubby, sandy areas.

🐾 Ticks

You won't be able to spend much time near the Carolina swamps without encountering ticks. All are nasty but the deer tick - no bigger than a pin head - carries with it the spectre of Lyme disease. Lyme disease attacks a dog's joints and makes walking painful. The tick needs to be embedded in the skin to transmit Lyme disease. It takes 4-6 hours for a tick to become embedded and another 24-48 hours to transmit Lyme disease bacteria.

When hiking, walk in the middle of trails away from tall grass and bushes. And when the summer sun fades away don't stop thinking about ticks - they remain active any time the temperature is above 30 degrees. By checking your dog - and yourself - thoroughly after each walk you can help avoid Lyme disease. Ticks tend to congregate on your dog's ears, between the toes and around the neck and head.

🐾 Water

Surface water, including fast-flowing streams, is likely to be infested with a microscopic protozoa called *Giardia*, waiting to wreak havoc on a dog's intestinal system. The most common symptom is crippling diarrhea. Algae, pollutants and contaminants can all be in streams, ponds and puddles. If possible, carry fresh water for your dog on the trail - your dog can even learn to drink happily from a squirt bottle.

At the beach, cool sea water will be tempting for your dog but try to limit any drinking as much as possible. Again, have plenty of fresh water available for your dog to drink instead.

Rattlesnakes and Copperheads, etc.

Rattlesnakes and their close cousins, copperheads, are not particularly aggressive animals but you should treat any venomous snake with respect and keep your distance. A rattler's colors may vary but they are recognized by the namesake rattle on the tail and a diamond-shaped head. Unless cornered or teased by humans or dogs, a rattlesnake will crawl away and avoid striking. Avoid placing your hand in unexamined rocky areas and crevasses and try and keep your dog from doing so as well. If you hear a nearby rattle, stop immediately and hold your dog back. Identify where the snake is and slowly back away.

If you or your dog is bitten, do not panic but get to a hospital or veterinarian with as little physical movement as possible. Wrap between the bite and the heart. Rattlesnakes might give "dry bites" where no poison is injected, but you should always check with a doctor after a bite even if you feel fine.

Black Bears

Are you likely to see a bear while out hiking with your dog? No, it's not likely. It is, however, quite a thrill if you are fortunate enough to spot a black bear on the trail - from a distance.

Black bear attacks are incredibly rare. In the year 2000 a hiker was killed by a black bear in Great Smoky National Park and it was the first deadly bear attack in the 66-year history of America's most popular national park. It was the first EVER in the southeastern United States. In all of North America only 43 black bear mauling deaths have ever been recorded (through 1999).

Most problems with black bears occur near a campground (like the above incident) where bears have learned to forage for unprotected food. On the trail bears will typically see you and leave the area. What should you do if you encounter a black bear? Experts agree on three important things:

1) Never run. A bear will outrun you, outclimb you, outswim you. Don't look like prey.
2) Never get between a female bear and a cub who may be nearby feeding.
3) Leave a bear an escape route.

If the bear is at least 15 feet away and notices you make sure you keep your dog close and calm. If a bear stands on its hind legs or comes closer it may just be trying to get a better view or smell to evaluate the situation. Wave your arms and make noise to scare the bear away. Most bears will quickly leave the area.

If you encounter a black bear at close range, stand upright and make yourself appear as large a foe as possible. Avoid direct eye contact and speak in a calm, assertive and assuring voice as you back up slowly and out of danger.

Alligators

Alligators are no longer endangered and range right through the Carolinas up through northeast North Carolina. Alligators are found in marshes, swamps, rivers and lakes as well as neighborhood drainage ditches and canals. Use common sense and do not not allow your dog in waters where alligators may be lurking. Don't walk your dog close to water if you can avoid it.

If you see an alligator on land, just walk your dog away from the alligator - alligators do not run down prey on land. They may run on land to escape danger or protect a nest but will not come after you if it has an escape route to the water. Make sure you give him one.

Outfitting Your Dog For A Hike

These are the basics for taking your dog on a hike:

▸ **Collar.**
It should not be so loose as to come off but you should be able to slide your flat hand under the collar.

▸ **Identification Tags.**
Get one with your veterinarian's phone number as well.

▸ **Bandanna.**
Can help distinguish him from game in hunting season.

▸ **Leash.**
Leather lasts forever but if there's water in your dog"s future, consider quick-drying nylon.

▸ **Water.**
Carry 8 ounces for every hour of hiking.

🐾 *I want my dog to help carry water, snacks and other supplies on the trail. Where do I start?*
To select an appropriate dog pack measure your dog's girth around the rib cage. A dog pack should fit securely without hindering the dog's ability to walk normally.

🐾 *Will my dog wear a pack?*
Wearing a dog pack is no more obtrusive than wearing a collar, although some dogs will take to a pack easier than others. Introduce the pack by draping a towel over your dog's back in the house and then having your dog wear an empty pack on short walks. Progressively add some crumpled newspaper and then bits of clothing. Fill the pack with treats and reward your dog from the stash. Soon your dog will associate the dog pack with an outdoor adventure and will eagerly look forward to wearing it.

⚫ *How much weight can I put into a dog pack?*

Many dog packs are sold by weight recommendations. A healthy, well-conditioned dog can comfortably carry 25% to 33% of its body weight. Breeds prone to back problems or hip dysplasia should not wear dog packs. Consult your veterinarian before stuffing the pouches with gear.

⚫ *How does a dog wear a pack?*

The pack, typically with cargo pouches on either side, should ride as close to the shoulders as possible without limiting movement. The straps that hold the dog pack in place should be situated where they will not cause chafing.

⚫ *What are good things to put in a dog pack?*

Low density items such as food and poop bags are good choices. Ice cold bottles of water can cool your dog down on hot days. Don't put anything in a dog pack that can break. Dogs will bang the pack on rocks and trees as they wiggle through tight spots in the trail. Dogs also like to lie down in creeks and other wet spots so seal items in plastic bags. A good use for dog packs when on day hikes around the Carolina coasts is trail maintenance - your dog can pack out trash left by inconsiderate visitors before you.

🐾 Are dog booties a good idea?

Dog booties can be an asset, especially for the occasional canine hiker whose paw pads have not become toughened. In some places, there may be broken glass. Hiking boots for dogs are designed to prevent pads from cracking while trotting across rough surfaces. Used in winter, dog booties provide warmth and keep ice balls from forming between toe pads when hiking through snow.

🐾 What should a doggie first aid kit include?

Even when taking short hikes it is a good idea to have some basics available for emergencies:

- 4" square gauze pads
- cling type bandaging tapes
- topical wound disinfectant cream
- tweezers
- insect repellent - no reason to leave your dog unprotected against mosquitoes and yellow flies
- veterinarian's phone number

"I can't think of anything that brings me closer to tears than when my old dog - completely exhausted after a hard day in the field - limps away from her nice spot in front of the fire and comes over to where I'm sitting and puts her head in my lap, a paw over my knee, and closes her eyes, and goes back to sleep. I don't know what I've done to deserve that kind of friend."
-Gene Hill

Low Impact Hiking With Your Dog

Every time you hike with your dog on the trail you are an ambassador for all dog owners. Some people you meet won't believe in your right to take a dog on the trail. Be friendly to all and make the best impression you can by practicing low impact hiking with your dog:

- Pack out everything you pack in.

- Do not leave dog scat on the trail; if you haven't brought plastic bags for poop removal bury it away from the trail and topical water sources.

- Hike only where dogs are allowed.

- Stay on the trail.

- Do not allow your dog to chase wildlife.

- Step off the trail and wait with your dog while horses and other hikers pass.

- Do not allow your dog to bark - people are enjoying the trail for serenity.

- *Have as much fun on your hike as your dog does.*

The Other End Of The Leash

Leash laws are like speed limits - everyone seems to have a private interpretation of their validity. Some dog owners never go outside with an unleashed dog; others treat the laws as suggestions or disregard them completely. It is not the purpose of this book to tell dog owners where to go to evade the leash laws or reveal the parks where rangers will look the other way at an unleashed dog. Nor is it the business of this book to preach vigilant adherence to the leash laws. Nothing written in a book is going to change people's behavior with regard to leash laws. So this will be the last time leash laws are mentioned, save occasionally when we point out the parks where dogs are welcomed off leash.

How To Pet A Dog
Tickling tummies slowly and gently works wonders.
Never use a rubbing motion; this makes dogs bad-tempered.
A gentle tickle with the tips of the fingers is all that is necessary
to induce calm in a dog. I hate strangers who go up to dogs with their
hands held to the dog's nose, usually palm towards themselves.
How does the dog know that the hand doesn't hold something horrid?
The palm should always be shown to the dog and go straight
down to between the dog's front legs and tickle gently with
a soothing voice to accompany the action.
Very often the dog raises its back leg in a scratching movement,
it gets so much pleasure from this.
-Barbara Woodhouse

No Dogs

Before we get started on the best places to take your dog, let's get out of the way some of the trails that do not allow dogs:

North Carolina
Currituck County Parks - all county parks
E-V Henwood Nature Preserve - Wilmington
Hoop Pole Creek Trail - Atlantic Beach
Nags Head Woods Preserve - Nags Head
Pea Island National Wildlife Refuge - Hatteras Island
Roosevelt Trail at North Carolina Aquarium - Bogue Banks

South Carolina
Cape Romain National Wildlife Refuge - Bull Island
Caw Caw Interpretive Center - Ravenal
Charles Towne Landing State Historic Site - Charleston
Pinckney Island National Wildlife Refuge - Hilton Head

O.K. that wasn't too bad. Let's forget about these and move on to some of the great places where we CAN take our dogs along the Carolina coasts...

10 Cool Things To See On Carolina Coastal Trails With Your Dog

"If your dog is fat," the old saying goes, "you aren't getting enough exercise." But walking the dog need not be just about a little exercise. Here are 10 cool things you can see on the Carolina coasts while out walking the dog.

🐾 PLACES YOU'VE SEEN ON THE SILVER SCREEN
Wilmington is often called "Hollywood East" and movie productions have made extensive use of the Carolina coastal scenery. The Vietnam scenes from *Forest Gump* were filmed in **Hunting Beach State Park**. The trees come right down to the beach and the lush, tropical feel of the vegetation indeed give off the aura of a jungle. A trail leads along the length of an inland lagoon where Forrest saved Lieutenant Dan. A few years later, Hunting Island doubled for Quang Tri Province in Vietnam when Samuel Jackson and Tommy Lee Jones showed up for *Rules of Engagement*. In 1982, Louis Jordan was a mad scientist trying to create new species at **Magnolia Plantation's Swamp Garden** in *Swamp Thing*. And if you hike with your dog along the *Sugarloaf Trail* in **Carolina Beach State Park** you might recognize some spots where corpse Terry Kiser did some water skiing in *Weekend at Bernie's*.

🐾 MYSTERIOUS OYSTER PILES
One of the most unique destinations of any trail on the Carolina coasts is the 12-foot high pile of oyster shells in **Edisto Beach State Park** on the *Spanish Mount Trail*. The oyster pile, known as a shell midden, is typical of American Indian rings found throughout the coastal islands. The Spanish Mount is estimated to be 4,000 years old, the second oldest known in South Carolina. These piles of bleached shells might have been built for ceremonies or possibly they are just ancient trash heaps.

HIGHEST SAND DUNES ON THE EAST COAST

It is one giant sandbox for your dog at **Jockey's Ridge State Park** on the Outer Banks, whose 90-foot dunes are the highest along the East Coast. Trails are laid out across the sand. On the mainland the *Sugarloaf Trail* in **Carolina Beach State Park** leads to a 50-foot sandpile that was often used as navigational aid in years gone by.

FAMOUS RESIDENCES

Archer Huntington designed his Moorish castle, Atalaya, in Murrells Inlet from memory after a trip to Spain. It can be seen today in **Huntington State Park**. The most spectacular home ever built on the Outer Banks was Edward Kinght's Corolla Island. He spent $400,000 on the Beaux Arts showcase in 1925 and it has been restored to its original splendor in **Currituck Heritage Park**. But the most-visited home on the Carolina coasts may be a World War II bunker in the dunes of **Fort Fisher State Recreation Area**. For 17 years the "Fort Fisher Hermit," Robert Herrill lived here. When word got out about Herrill's lifestyle, so many people came to hear his philosophies of life that North Carolina officials called him the state's second largest tourist attraction behind only the battleship *North Carolina*.

900 DIFFERENT CAMELLIAS

The extremely dog-friendly **Magnolia Plantation** gives your dog a rare chance to hike through a formal garden, one of America's oldest. Besides the 900 varieties of camellias on display the Charleston garden is planted with over 250 types of azaleas.

PREHISTORIC CANOES

Over the years 29 prehistoric Algonquian Indian canoes have been uncovered in **Pettigrew State Park's** Lake Phelps, preserved in the shallow waters. The canoes were fashioned by burning straight cypress logs over a slow fire and scraping away the charred sections. They were stored for the winter in the muds of the lake. Two are on display in the park - one from 380 A.D. and the other 1440 A.D.

SPECTACULAR LIGHTHOUSES

There are five lighthouses on the Outer Banks your dog can visit - three in the **Cape Hatteras National Seashore**. The oldest operating lighthouse in North Carolina is the 75-foot tower on Ocracoke Island and the 150-foot Bodie Island Lighthouse dates to 1872. The most famous, and America's tallest at 208 feet, is the black-and-white swirl-striped Cape Hatteras Lighthouse. In South Carolina your dog can trot around the only public light in the Palmetto State at **Hunting Island State Park**.

ANIMAL EATING PLANTS

At several locations along the Carolina coasts your dog can hike through the unique habitats of pocosins, boglands called by the Indian term for "swamp on a hill." Plants living in these nutrient-poor soilshave evolved to trap insects and digest them in lethal juices. Such killers as Venus' Fly Traps, blatterworts and sundews can be seen in North Carolina in **Carolina Beach State Park** and in South Carolina in the **Audubon-Newhall Preserve**, among others.

FORTS, FORTS AND MORE FORTS

Starting with the first English earthworks in the New World at **Fort Raleigh**, the defense of coastal Carolina has always been a military priority. Your dog can examine the defensive earthworks at **Moores Creek**, site of a critical American victory during the Revolution, and hike through the Civil War masonry bastion at **Fort Macon**. Or the more primitive Civil War earthworks at Fort **Lamar**. For a look at modern fortification, take the dog to Battery Jasper at **Fort Moultrie** - but don't be disappointed if he's more interested in the beach.

🐾 OLD MINES

The lowcountry was once an ancient seabed, a vast graveyard for millions of years of sea creatures. These marine deposits near the soil surface contain phosphate and calcium, minerals valuable in cement making and for fertilizing fields. The minerals were enthusiastically mined in the 1800s and phosphate mines brought prosperity to towns devastated by the Civil War. The **Edisto Nature Trail** leads to an old mining site and processing plant where phosphate was loaded on barges and shipped down-river to Charleston.

The 50 Best Places
To Hike With Your
Dog On The Carolina
Coasts...

1
Hunting Island
State Park

The Park

The 5000-acre island was once a hunting preserve, hence its name. Before that it was a stopover for sailors and pirates. Much of the park was developed as a Depression-era project and its 1120-foot fishing pier is one of the longest on the East Coast.

The lighthouse in the park, built in 1859 and destroyed in the Civil War before being rebuilt with cast iron plates designed to be dismantled and moved, is the only public light in South Carolina. When open, you can climb the 167 steps - without your dog - to the top for a commanding view of the shoreline.

The Walks

Hunting Island State Park is one of the best places you can bring your dog. Dogs are allowed on the park trails and the ocean beach - four miles of natural sand - is open for long canine hikes beside the Atlantic waves.

The formal trails include a one-mile nature trail near the lighthouse and a 4-mile long hiking trail that travels on parallel courses deep into the island.

Colleton

Phone Number
- (843) 838-2011

Website
- www.southcarolinaparks.com/park-finder/state-park/1019.aspx

Admission Fee
- Yes, per person

Hours
- Sat-Th 6:00 a.m.-6:00 p.m.; Fri 6:00 a.m.-8:00 p.m. (hours extended to 10:00 p.m. daily during Daylight Savings Time)

Directions
- *Hunting Island*; take US 17 to Gardens Corner, then take a left on Highway 21 to the park.

Both are easy going for you and your dog. The surface is sandy and easy on the paw. Extended hiking is available on some of the lightly traveled roads, service roads and bike paths. As a side trip, a marsh boardwalk has been constructed over a salt water marsh overlooking Johnson Creek.

You will find an abundance of cabbage palmetto forests - the South Carolina state tree - on the island. Although the palms form a thick canopy it will get hot at Hunting Island and there are few fresh water sources so make sure you bring water for your dog when hiking here. The dog-friendly campground is only a few steps from the beach.

Trail Sense: There are informational kiosks at the trailhead and a park map is available.

The Hunting Island light is the only lighthouse in South Carolina open to the public.

Dog Friendliness

Dogs are welcome across the park.

Traffic

This is South Carolina's most popular park - more than a million visitors a year so there will be times of the year when the trails will be noisier than others.

Canine Swimming

As much as your dog wants in the Atlantic Ocean.

Trail Time

More than one hour.

2
Cape Hatteras National Seashore

The Park

Cape Hatteras National Seashore stretches down the Outer Banks for 70 sandy miles across three barrier islands, two connected by a toll-free bridge and two connected by a free ferry. Today the seashore is known for its recreational opportunities on the land; historically it has been known for its dangers offshore. A bank of shifting sands known as the Diamond Shoals have caused more than 600 ships to wreck off Cape Hatteras, leading mariners to call the area the "Graveyard of the Atlantic."

Cape Hatteras was designated America's first National Seashore by Congress on August 17, 1937 and established on January 12, 1953.

Dare
Phone Number - (252) 473-2111
Website - www.nps.gov/caha
Admission Fee - None
Park Hours - Daylight hours
Directions - *Outer Banks*; along Route 12 from the intersection with Route 64 at Whalebone Junction south through Ocracoke Island.

The Walks

There is no better place for *loooong* hikes with your dog on dune-backed beaches than Cape Hatteras National Seashore but there are also a trio of short nature trails - one on each island - to try with your dog.

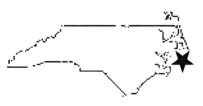

The best of the lot is in Buxton Woods on Hatteras Island, near the Visitor Center and lighthouse. This trail bounds across pine and oak-covered dunes with marshy wetlands tossed into the mix. The gnarled trees and shrub thickets provide a shady respite from a day on the beach with your dog.

Another leafy canine hike is on the *Hammock Hills Nature Trail* on Ocracoke Island which traipses through a maritime forest on the edge of Pamlico Sound for a bit less than a mile. For an easy hike with your dog in the sunshine

and salt air stop at Bodie Island Lighthouse. Here you can explore freshwater ponds and marshes that were artificially created by building dams and dikes and artificial dunes to block the intrusion of ocean salt spray.

Trail Sense: A park map is available to find the trailheads and the trails are well-marked.

The current location of the Hatteras Light is not the original - in 1999 the entire 208-foot structure was moved a half-mile away from the encroaching ocean. The journey took 23 days.

Dog Friendliness

Dogs are permitted year-round in the national seashore, save for three small swimming areas.

Traffic

You can find a desolate stretch of beach or trail most times you seek them.

Canine Swimming

If your dog is intimidated by the crashing Atlantic surf there is also access to Pamlico Sound.

Trail Time

More than an hour - days if you want.

3
Huntington Beach State Park

The Park

The land for this park was once part of the 10,000-acre Brookgreen Gardens created by Archer Huntington, step-son of Collis P. Huntington, one of the builders of the Transcontinental Railroad. He purchased the former rice plantation to display the works of his wife, sculptor Anna Hyatt and others. When it was opened in 1932 Brookgreen was the country's first public sculpture garden.

Huntington State Park, which includes about 2,500 acres - mostly marshlands - was founded in 1960.

Horry

Phone Number
- (843) 237-4440

Website
- www.southcarolinaparks.com/park-finder/state-park/1020.aspx

Admission Fee
- Yes, per person

Park Hours
- Sat-Th 6:00 a.m.-6:00 p.m.; Fri 6:00 a.m.-8:00 p.m. (hours extended to 10:00 p.m. daily during Daylight Savings Time)

Directions
- *Murrells Inlet*; three miles south of town on the ocean side of US 17.

The Walks

There are two formal trails here, both completely contained under a maritime forest. The *Kerrigan Nature Trail* is a short planks-and-pine straw affair that leads to an overlook of the freshwater lagoon (the saltwater marsh can be viewed via an elevated boardwalk). The one canine hikers will want to sample most is the *Sandpiper Pond Trail*, a rolling, sandy romp past an interdune pond. The Atlantic Ocean beach can be used to close a 2-mile loop on this out-and-back trail. Viewing platforms are spaced along the route that serve as ideal resting spots for your dog after trotting through thick sand.

For many dogs the best part of Huntington State Park will be the three miles of undeveloped beach. To leave the sunbathers behind park at the boardwalk and head north on the beach. You will reach a jetty in 1.2 miles.

Trail Sense: The trailheads are easy to find but things can get confusing on the *Sandpiper Pond Trail* with its spurs to the beach and campground. You will see red-topped poles sort of marking the way but you can also see some in the bushes as well.

Dog Friendliness
Dogs are allowed on the park trails, on the beach and in the campground.

Traffic
There is plenty of room to spread out on the beach and the nature trails are overlooked by most visitors.

Canine Swimming
The Atlantic Ocean will fill the bill nicely.

Trail Time
Many hours, if your dog wants.

4
Merchants Millpond
State Park

The Park

Settlement in Gates County - named for Horatio Gates of Revolutionary War fame - began in the 1660s and millponds were built to process and market regional produce. The Merchants Millpond was constructed in 1811 and supported a sawmill, gristmills and a farm supply store making this the center of trade in the county.

Milling continued in the area for over 100 years until World War II when much of the land was sold to developers. A local outdoorsman, A.B. Coleman, though the area too beautiful to be altered by bulldozers and purchased the property in the 1960s. He donated 919 acres that led to the establishment of Merchants Millpond State Park in 1973. Additional donations have swelled the park's size to over 3,000 acres.

Gates

Phone Number
- (252) 357-1191

Website
- http://ils.unc.edu/parkproject/visit/memi/home.html

Admission Fee
- None

Hours
- Open 8:00 a.m. every day; closes 6:00 p.m. Nov-Feb, 7:00 p.m. Mar and Oct, 8:00 p.m. Apr-May and Sep, 9:00 p.m. Jun-Aug

Directions
- *Gatesville;* four miles east of town on US 158. The park entrance is just east of the intersection with NC 37 and eight miles west of NC 32.

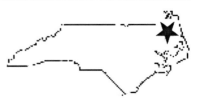

The Walks

The longest loop of pure canine hiking on the Carolina coasts can be found here - the 6.7-mile *Lassiter Trail.* This is easy going for your dog on soft, pine straw-littered paths. Wooden bridges tame the wilder stretches. Your dog will happily leave the long, flat stretches at the shore for the gentle hillocks in Merchants Millpond State Park, bounding up eagerly to discover what awaits on the other side.

Much of the character of the eerie "enchanted forest" of the Lassiter Swamp comes from the mistletoe that has twisted and gnarled the branches of tupelo gum trees into fantastic shapes.

Identified nearly 2000 years ago, Anglo Saxons named the plant "mistle-tan" meaning "dung twig" after bird droppings on a branch. It was thought the plant's existence was entwined with birds but it is actually a parasitic plant that is also known as the Vampire Plant. The mistletoe sends out a root-like structure into the bark of hardwood trees and extracts all its nutrients from its host. The mistletoe's mooching won't kill the tupelo gum - if the host dies, it dies. You can recognize mistletoe by its clumps of 2-inch greenish-yellow leaves and clusters of white berries.

The tradition of kissing under a sprig of mistletoe dates back hundreds of years. The proper procedure is to pick one berry off the plant for every kiss received. When the berries are gone, so are the kisses. Make sure you dispose of the berries after you're through bussing - they are toxic to dogs and people.

The star of the park is the 760-acre millpond that harbors ancient bald cypress and tupelo gum trees. But out on the trail you'll be hiking under a pleasant mix of pines and hardwoods such as American beech.

If your dog is not up for a three-hour hiking loop, sign on to the *Coleman Loop*, a two-miler that touches the southern shore of the millpond. You can access the *Coleman Trail* at the canoe launch on NC 37 and this is a wonderful place to canoe with your dog as well.

Trail Sense: Grab a park map - the trails are self-revealing but all are marked by white blazes which can cause momentary confusion.

Dog Friendliness
Dogs are welcome on the trails and in the campground.

Traffic
This is a popular park but the crowds slip away as you cross the *Fire Trail* and get deep towards the Lassiter Swamp.

Canine Swimming
There are places for your dog to slip into the dark waters of the millpond.

Trail Time
Several hours available.

5
Jockey's Ridge
State Park

The Park

Jockey's Ridge, with heights varying from 80 to 100 feet, is the tallest natural sand dune system on the Atlantic seacoast. The vast expanse of sand stays in place due to the shifting winds that blow the massive sand pile back one way and then back the other.

Once discovered, the naked hilltops served as an important navigational landmark for European explorers. Its name is though to survive from wild pony races staged in the flats at the base of the dune.

As access to the Outer Banks barrier islands increased after World War II development pressures galvanized local groups into action to save the dunes. In 1974 Jockey's Ridge was designated a National Natural Landmark. The state park began taking shape the next year and today encompasses 420 acres.

Dare

Phone Number
- (252) 441-7132

Website
- www.jockeysridgestatepark.com

Admission Fee
- None

Park Hours
- Open at 8:00 a.m. every day; closes at 6:00 p.m. Nov-Feb, 7:00 p.m. Mar anOct, 8:00 p.m. Apr, May and Sept, 9:00 p.m. Jun-Aug

Directions
- *Nags Head*; at Milepost 12 on the South Croatan Highway (Route 158 Bypass) on the Outer Banks.

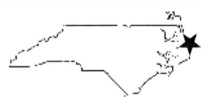

The Walks

This is the closest thing you will find to mountain-climbing for your dog on the Carolina coasts - all on sand. Your dog is welcome to play anywhere throughout this vast sand box. The soft sands, steep dunes and stiff winds can make for invigorating canine hiking at Jockey's Ridge. And avoid the middle of a summer day - the sands can be as much as 30 degrees hotter than the air temperature and can burn a dog's paw pads.

For dogs who like their walking more structured there are two interpretive nature trails marked by posts across the dunes. The 1.5-mile *Tracks in the Sand*

Trail departs from the Visitor's Center and highlights the signs in the sand left by small mammals, reptiles, birds, insects and even plants that have adapted to this desert environment. The 1-mile *Soundside Overlook Trail* explores the four different environments of the park including shrub forest and brackish marsh. Both trails lead to the sandy edge of the Roanoke Sound estuary where the gentle waters make an ideal canine swimming pool - or a cool walkway through the shallows.

Trail Sense: A park map is available and the trails are well-marked by wooden signposts and the pawprints of those dogs that have gone before you.

Dog Friendliness

Dogs are allowed throughout the park.

Traffic

Foot traffic only and there is seldom any need to follow another dog's paw-prints.

Canine Swimming

If your dog finds the Roanoke Sound waters too tame the Atlantic Ocean is only a couple of blocks away - and dogs are allowed on the Nags Head beach year-round.

Trail Time

More than one hour.

It may only be 90 feet to the top of Jockey's Ridge but your dog may still want to stop for a rest or two on the way up.

6
Edisto Beach
State Park

The Park

Rice and indigo were the first cash crops when Edisto Island was founded in the late 1600s but it was Sea Island Cotton that brought fame and fortune. It is reliably stated that the Pope once insisted that his garments be made only of Edisto Island cotton.

The War Between the States and the boll weevil destroyed the cotton fields while island residents turned to truck farming by the end of the 19th century. In the 20th century development came slowly. During the Depression, the Civilian Conservation Corps built the 1,255-acre park on land donated by the Edisto Company in 1935.

Colleton

Phone Number
- (843) 869-2756

Website
- www.southcarolinaparks.com/park-finder/state-park/1298.aspx

Admission Fee
- Yes, per person

Park Hours
- Sat-Th 6:00 a.m.-6:00 p.m.; Fri 6:00 a.m.-8:00 p.m. (hours extended to 10:00 p.m. daily during Daylight Savings Time)

Directions
- *Edisto Beach*; from US 17 head south on Route 174 for 28 miles to the town and park.

The Walks

The standout canine hike at Edisto Beach is the *Spanish Mount Trail* that leads from the Live Oak Campground to one of the earliest known American Indian shell mound sites. The wooded trail is 1.7 miles one way and moves along a wide hard-packed dirt road. You can avoid completely retracing your

pawprints on the return trip by using the *Forest Loop Trail* or the *Scott Creek Trail*. All the canine hiking here is on natural surfaces and easy going.

When your dog gets his fill of the hiking in the woods along Scott Creek - and you'll find some of South Carolina's tallest palmetto trees here - head next

One of the most unique destinations of any trail on the Carolina coasts is the 12-foot high pile of oyster shells on the *Spanish Mount Trail*. The oyster pile, known as a shell midden, is typical of American Indian rings found throughout the coastal islands. The Spanish Mount is estimated to be 4,000 years old, the second oldest known in South Carolina. These piles of bleached shells might have been built for ceremonies or possibly they are just ancient trash heaps.

for the Atlantic Ocean and the park's 1.5 miles of beachfront. If she still isn't tired you can keep hiking on the sand into adjoining Edisto Beach, which has remained a residential beach.

Trail Sense: There are informational kiosks at the trailhead and a park map is available.

Dog Friendliness

Dogs are allowed on the park trails, on the beach and in the campgrounds but not in the cabins.

Traffic

This is one of South Carolina's most popular parks but the trails lead away from most of the activity.

Canine Swimming

Absoultely, in the Atlantic Ocean.

Trail Time

Many hours.

There is enough canine hiking in Edisto Beach State Park to tire any dog.

7
Fort Fisher State Recreation Area

The Park

The largest earthwork fort in the Confederacy was constructed here to keep Wilmington open to blockade runners during the Civil War. Until July 1862, Fort Fisher was little more than several sand batteries mounting fewer than two dozen guns. Colonel William Lamb, working on designs created in Russia for the Crimean War, employed as many as 1,000 men, many of them slaves, to create one mile of sea defense and one-third of a mile of land defense.

The Union had long planned an assault on Fort Fisher but did not feel confident to do so until December 24, 1864. For two days the sand and earth fortifications absorbed Union shells and the force withdrew. On January 12 the fort was bombarded by land and sea and finally capitulated after six hours of fierce fighting. It was considered the greatest land-sea battle of the Civil War and helped seal the ultimate fate of the Confederacy.

New Hanover

Phone Number
- (910) 458-5798

Website
- http://ils.unc.edu/parkproject/visit/fofi/home.html

Admission Fee
- None

Park Hours
- Open 24 hours a day

Directions
- *Kure Beach;* from Wilmington follow US 421 South. Five miles south of Carolina Beach turn left on Loggerhead Road into the recreation area.

The Walks

Most canine hikers will bring their dogs to Fort Fisher for its seven miles of tail-friendly white sand beaches. Head south from the Visitor Center and you will discover nothing but open, dune-backed beach ahead of you.

But there are a couple of fun options here as well. The *Basin Trail* slips almost unnoticed from the south end of the parking lot into what appears to be a maritime forest. You twist through a maze of wax myrtles for only a few steps, however, before bursting into the open with nothing but a flat expanse of sand in every direction. Forging on, you cross a marsh and soon bring your dog to an old World War II bunker. Further on, your destination is a a platform overlooking The Basin a half-mile away.

On the north boundary of the park is the Fort Fisher State Historic Site where you can hike among the formidable earthwork mounds that give a clear view of the Cape Fear River and the strategic importance of the site. A captured cannon and relics recovered from sunken blockade runners are among the tresures on display.

Trail Sense: A park map/brochure allows you to navigate tot he major attractions in the park.

Dog Friendliness
Dogs are allowed across Fort Fisher except in the swimming areas or the changing facilities.
Traffic
The further you hike from the Visitor Center the less you'll find.
Canine Swimming
Of course, in the Atlantic Ocean.
Trail Time
A full day is possible.

8
Magnolia Plantation and Gardens

The Park

For Thomas Drayton and his son, Thomas, Jr., in 1675 it was Barbados or bust. They boarded the ship *Willing Wind* and left England only to arrive in what had become the most densely populated colony in the British empire. With all the choice land for a sugar plantation already snapped up the Draytons turned their attention to the new Carolina Colony.

Soon after arriving on the Ashley River young Drayton married Ann Fox and inherited the Magnolia Plantation in 1680. The young couple set about building a plantation house and at the same time planted America's first estate garden, Flowerdale.

Through the Revolution and the Civil War and the end of the age of the gentleman planter the estate was ravaged but the gardens survived intact. In the 1870s, Magnolia Gardens opened to the visitors as one of the country's oldest public gardens. Today the estate remains in the hands of the Drayton family and Flowerdale looks much as it did 300-plus years ago.

Charleston

Phone Number
- (843) 571-1266

Website
- www.magnoliaplantation.com/index.html

Admission Fee
- Yes, per person

Park Hours
- 8:00 a.m. to dusk

Directions
- *Charleston*; on Ashley River Road (SC 61). From US 17 go west for ten miles.

The Walks

You wouldn't expect to find a formal garden in a guidebook of places to hike with your dog. But how dog-friendly is Magnolia Plantation? Not only are dogs allowed to walk the grounds but they can ride the tour trams and even go in the plantation house (if you carry the dog). And it is quite a treat - you are not likely to have a canine hike like this anywhere else. The prescribed path through the maze of walking paths stops at two dozen points of interest, crosses graceful bridges, looks in on 250 varieties of azaleas, skips through quiet stands of towering bamboo and wanders by 900 types of camellias.

The cypress knees that sprout from the baldcypress trees make a handy hitching post for your dog.

More hiking with your dog is available through the 60-acre blackwater cypress and tupelo swamp. Plus there are nature trails on the property.

Trail Sense: Signs and maps and guides show the way.

Dog Friendliness

As dog-friendly as a major tourist attraction can be.

Traffic

Although there are always plenty of folks in the gardens you will often find yourself alone among the lush plantings.

Canine Swimming

Land-loving dogs only.

Trail Time

More than one hour.

9
Carolina Beach State Park

The Park

Hostilities with the local Cape Fear Indians caused settlement to come slowly to this region. The small tribe was driven away in 1725 and a small English town established. The British designated Cape Fear as one of its five official Colonial ports of entry and the economic fortunes of the locals brightened accordingly.

The peninsula became an island in 1929 with the dredging of Snow's Cut for the Intracoastal Waterway. The state of North Carolina recognized the unique environment at the junction of the waterway and Cape Fear River and in 1969 spent its first money for a park since the purchase of Mount Mitchell in 1916. Carolina Beach State Park - named for the town since it is not on the ocean - was established that same year.

The Walks

Carolina Beach State Park boasts one of the most extensive trail systems on the Carolina coasts. The feature canine hike among a half-dozen named paths is the *Sugarloaf Trail* that leads to a 55-foot high pile of sand on the bank of the Cape Fear River. Sugarloaf Dune appeared on navigational charts as early as 1738 and was an important landmark for river pilots. The Confederacy also made use of the dune during the Civil War, stationing 5,000 troops near here as part of the defense of Wilmington.

New Hanover

Phone Number
- (910) 458-8206

Website
- http://ils.unc.edu/parkproject/visit/cabe/home.html

Admission Fee
- None

Park Hours
- Open 8:00 a.m. every day; closes 6:00 p.m. Nov-Feb, 7:00 p.m. Mar and Oct, 8:00 p.m. Apr-May and Sep, 9:00 p.m. Jun-Aug

Directions
- *Carolina Beach*; after driving across the Intracoastal Waterway on the Snow's Cut Bridge turn right at the second stoplight onto Dow Road. The park is on the right on State Park Road.

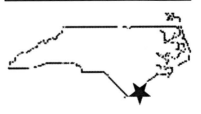

There is plenty of room for your dog to stretch out on the inviting Carolina Beach State Park trails.

The *Sugarloaf Trail* winds for three miles through a typical Southern forest of pines and live oaks and eventually leads to a triad of ponds, each with its own personality. All told there are six miles of sandy, paw-friendly trails here.

Trail Sense: A park map is available and notices are posted about trail closures due to hurricane damage. The trails are well-blazed.

Dog Friendliness
Dogs are allowed on the trails and in the campground.

Traffic
The trails are open to foot traffic only.

Canine Swimming
There are places in the Cape Fear River for your dog to cool off.

Trail Time
Several hours on these flat, easy to walk trails.

10
Myrtle Beach State Park

The Park

Franklin G. Burroughs controlled a 19th century turpentine and naval stores empire in Horry County, owning much of the land east of Conway. It was always his dream to run a railroad to the coast and develop a resort town almost exactly halfway between New York City and Miami.

Burroughs died in 1897 before he could follow through on his plans but his heirs built that railroad and created the Myrtle Beach Farms (named for the dominant species of tree in the area) real estate company in 1912. In 1934, in the 100th anniversary year of Franklin Burrough's birth, the company donated the land for what would become South Carolina's first state park. Myrtle Beach State Park opened formally on July 1, 1936.

The Walks

The star hike in the park is the one-mile *Sculptured Oak Trail* that snakes through a 100-acre remnant of maritime forest. This is easy traveling for your dog

Horry
Phone Number - (843) 238-5325
Website - www.southcarolinaparks.com/park-finder/state-park/795.aspx
Admission Fee - Yes, per person
Park Hours - 6:00 a.m. to 10:00 p.m.
Directions - *Myrtle Beach*; the park is at 4401 South Kings Highway, four miles south of town on Business 17.

on soft natural surfaces and a shady respite from the hot beach. A short spur leads to a small woodland pond where you can observe some of the more than 200 species of birds that have been recorded here.

Additional canine hiking in this slice of forest - designated a Heritage Trust site - can be found on the red-blazed *Yaupon Trail*. The two trails both spill out of the woods at the park's mile-long stretch of Atlantic Ocean beach. You can hike the wide sand beach as far as your dog wishes but only the beach in the park is dune-backed.

Trail Sense: A park map/brochure is available and the trailhead is marked by wooden signs. On the trail, colored posts and junction signs keep you heading in the right direction.

Dog Friendliness

Dogs are allowed year-round on the beach, on the trails and in the campground. Dogs are not permitted in or around the cabins.

Traffic

This is one of South Carolina's most popular parks, attracting more than one million visitors each year.

Canine Swimming

Absolutely.

Trail Time

More than an hour.

11

Mt. Pleasant Palmetto Islands County Park

The Park

The unique park was originally designed on and around 140 acres of tidal wetlands, marsh, sand barrens, and 16 spotted islands, some as small as three-tenths acre and the largest being 26 acres. As the park expanded into a busy 943 recreational acres with a playground and splash park it retains its naural feel thanks to its thick tropical plantings.

The Walks

The marquee trail here is the *Nature Island Trail* reached by an open boardwalk across a salt marsh. The island was energetically logged through the mid-1900s although it is hard to tell these days. This canine hike is on planks and pine straw that your dog will love under the palmetto, loblolly pine and live oak trees.

Back on the main island you can pick up various hard-packed multi-use trails that connect picnic shelters and skirts the salt marsh. Most of these paths, including the *Osprey Nature Trail,* pass maze-like through the walls of vegetation.

Charleston

Phone Number
- (843) 884-0832

Website
- www.ccprc.com/index.asp?NID=69

Admission Fee
- $1.00

Park Hours
- Open 9:00 a.m. every day; closes at 5:00 p.m. Nov-Feb, 6:00 p.m. Mar-Apr, 7:00 p.m. May-Aug, 6:00 p.m. Sept-Oct

Directions
- *Mount Pleasant*; west of US 17. Turn onto Long Point Road south of the junction with Route 41 and north of Route 517. Continue past Charles Pinckney NHS to Needlerush Parkway and turn right. Follow road to the park at end.

This wide boardwalk leads your dog onto Nature Island at Mt. Pleasant Palmetto Islands County Park.

The center of the park has been cleared for a large meadow that is reserved for unstructured play, like a game of fetch.

Trail Sense: An accurate trail map and signposts direct your explorations.

Dog Friendliness

Dogs are allowed throughout the park.

Traffic

This is a busy place but you can leave most of the action behind when you hike over to Nature Island.

Canine Swimming

Your dog can find some aquatics in Horlbeck Creek.

Trail Time

More than one hour.

12

Goose Creek State Park

The Park

Long an isolated area of logging and commercial fishing, local citizens here began agitating North Carolina for a state park in the early 1970s. More than 1,200 acres of land were purchased along Goose Creek and the park opened in September, 1974. Today Goose Creek State Park contains 1,667 acres.

The Walks

A diverse trail system at Goose Creek State Park is built around the many creeks that lubricate the property. The *Ivey Gut* and *Goose Creek* trails are the main thoroughfares through the evergreens and hardwoods that are pinched by marshes and swamps. Most of your dog's steps on these paths will fall on paw-friendly sandy dirt.

Other trails that trace the paths of slow-moving creeks tend to be gooey and rooty. These pathways are aided by crushed stone and boardwalks when needed.

The centerpiece trail in the park is the *Palmetto Boardwalk Trail* that travels over a hardwood swamp. All told there are seven miles of trails here but most of the routes are one-way so you can spend quite a bit of time on these quiet, unhurried trails with your dog.

Trail Sense: There is a park map and brochure and some of the trails have

Beaufort

Phone Number
- (252) 923-2191

Website
- http://ils.unc.edu/parkproject/visit/gocr/do.html

Admission Fee
- None

Hours
- Open 8:00 a.m. every day; closes 6:00 p.m. Nov-Feb, 7:00 p.m. Mar and Oct, 8:00 p.m. Apr-May and Sep, 9:00 p.m. Jun-Aug

Directions
- *Washington;* 10 miles east of town on the north side of the Pamlico River. From US 264 turn south on Camp Leach Road for 2.5 miles to the park on the right.

The end of the line on the Flatty Creek Trail.

Dog Friendliness

Dogs are permitted on the trails and in the campground.

Traffic

The trails are foot traffic only and lightly traveled.

Canine Swimming

A sandy beach on the Pamlico River is an ideal canine swimming hole when the park is not crowded.

Trail Time

More than one hour.

13
Pettigrew State Park

The Park

James Johnston Pettigrew was born here on the shore of Lake Phelps on Independence Day in 1828. He entered the University of North Carolina at the age of fourteen and was valedictorian four years later. His commencement address was so impressve that President James Polk, who was in attendance, offered him a professorship at the United States Naval Observatory.

Pettigrew went on to practice law, author books and dabble in South Carolina politics. Active in the militia, he served as a Colonel in the early days of the Civil War in the taking of Fort Sumter. Returning to his native North Carolina, Pettigrew became a brigadier general leading his regiment to the furthest Southern advance at Gettysburg.

General Pettigrew survived the action on the Gettysburg battlefield but was mortally wounded in the retreat. He is buried in the park, named in his honor in 1939. His grave is reached on the *Cemetery Trail*.

Washington/Tyrell

Phone Number
- (252) 797-4475

Website
- http://ils.unc.edu/parkproject/visit/pett/home.html

Admission Fee
- None

Park Hours
- Open 8:00 a.m. every day; closes 6:00 p.m. Nov-Feb, 7:00 p.m. Mar and Oct, 8:00 p.m. Apr-May and Sep, 9:00 p.m. Jun-Aug

Directions
- *Creswell*; seven miles south of town off US 64. Go through town, following signs to Lake Shore Road and the park.

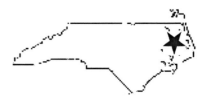

The Walks

The canine hiking at Pettigrew State Park runs in a narrow band around Lake Phelps, the second largest natural lake in North Carolina. There are about eight miles of segmented one-way linear trails along the north shore of the lake.

Near the park office the *Bee Tree Trail* runs through Somerset Place State Historic Site, an interpretive plantation dating to the late 1700s. Pushing out to the west, the 2.8-mile *Moccasin Trail* heads for the Moccasin Overlook, considered the most scenic spot in the park where every tree is decorated in strands of Spanish moss.

The final 4.2 miles of the park on Lake Phelps is covered by the *Morotoc Trail*, a multi-use path. All your dog's hiking in the

Every dog gets his picture snapped in this Pettigrew State Park tree.

park is flat, easy going on soft - sometimes muddy - naural surfaces. Except for Somerset Place most of the trails move through a canopy of light woods.

Trail Sense: A park map is available for orientation.

Dog Friendliness
Dogs are welcome throughout the park.

Traffic
Bikes are allowed on some trails; there are certainly long stetches of trail where you can expect to be alone with your dog.

Canine Swimming
Access to Lake Phelps is not always easy; the boat ramp near the office may be your best bet for spirited canine aquatics.

Trail Time
Without a car shuttle, you can spend all day hiking with your dog from Bee Tree Overlook to Cypress Point and back.

14
Edisto
Nature Trail

The Park

The Edisto Nature Trail is the public face of MeadWestvaco's forest management practices. The paper and packaging products company opened the trail to the public in 1976.

The Walks

This is the best interpretive nature trail on the Carolina coasts. Subtle changes in moisture and elevation in this typical Lowcountry setting conspire to produce a wide variety of trees from live oaks emblematic of the South to the yellow poplars that are the tallest trees in northern deciduous forests. A detailed booklet explains it all across this 1.5-mile stacked loop system on the edge of the Edisto River Swamp.

This is easy hiking for your dog on soft - sometimes gooey - natural surfaces and occasional boardwalks. Some of those pawprints will be left on some of South Carolina's most historic traverses. You start on traces of the Old Charleston Road, authorized in 1737 and traveled by George Washington.

Colleton

Phone Number
- None

Website
- www.sctrails.net/trails/ALL-TRAILS/NRT/EdistoNature.html

Admission Fee
- None

Hours
- Sunrise to sunset

Directions
- *Jacksonboro*; on US 17 (the north side), just east of town. The parking lot is on the south side of the Edisto River bridge.

Later your dog will trot on a bit of the King's Highway that is even older. It was developed to link Charles Towne (today's Charleston) and Savannah between 1670 and 1733. The back of the main loop utilizes an old railroad bed. The entire route is shaded under the canopy of a mature woodland.

Trail Sense: The trail is blazed with yellow triangles and an excellent trail guide is available at the trailhead.

Dog Friendliness

Dogs are allowed on the *Edisto Nature Trail* - a happy pair of hiking dogs are featured on the website.

Traffic

Foot traffic only but don't expect to see any.

Canine Swimming

None.

Trail Time

About one hour.

15
Dungannon Plantation Heritage Preserve

The Park

Rice will not grow in saltwater. When the rice culture developed in South Carolina in the late 18th century hundreds of earthen dikes were built to block tidal streams and create fresh-water ponds. Dungannon Plantation, named for Dungannon Township in Ireland, was one such working plantation.

This 643-acre tract was purchased in 1995 by the South Carolina Department of Natural Resources Heritage Trust Program to protect one of the state's largest nesting sites of the federally-endangered wood stork. About half the preserve consists of the impounded cypress and tupelo swamp.

Charleston

Phone Number
- None

Website
- www.dnr.sc.gov/managed/ heritage/dungannon/description.html

Admission Fee
- None

Park Hours
- Daylight to dusk

Directions
- *Hollywood*; east of town on Route 162. From US 17 take Route 165 South in Ravenel to the intersection with Route 162 and turn left. The parking lot will be on the left.

The Walks

For the pure experience of getting out in the woods and hiking with your dog you won't find a better spot on the Carolina coasts than Dungannon Plantation. There are about five miles of designated nature trails on wide woods roads and single-file secondary trails.

All the canine hiking here is under a light, airy forest. This was once the habitat of longleaf pine but most were harvested long ago to be replaced by red maple and sweet gum. Their leaves blanket the trails and sometimes hide a rooty path. Some of these secondary routes can get squishy under paw but the moist areas support a dizzying array of wildflowers. Five species of orchid can be seen on the Preserve.

Trail Sense: A trail map is available at an informational kiosk and metal hiking disks are placed at most trail junctions out in the woods.

Your dog will find the woods at Dungannon Plantation Heritage Preserve are expansive and airy.

Dog Friendliness

Dogs are permitted to hike these wooded trails.

Traffic

No motorized vehicles or horses are allowed and most days you can hike with your dog for hours without seeing another trail user.

Canine Swimming

No swimming for your dog in the swamp - there are alligators present.

Trail Time

More than one hour.

16
Patsy Pond
Nature Trail

The Park

Patsy Pond Nature Trail is located along the southern boundary of the Croatan National Forest and managed by the North Carolina Coastal Federation which safeguards the state's coastal rivers, creeks, sounds and beaches.

The Walks

The trail system here is comprised of a trio of loops - an inner and an outer circle each accessed by an introductory loop. This is easy, pleasant trotting for your dog on sandy paths through an airy pine forest with only scattered understory. The forest is so open that the trees cannot block out the droning traffic noise from Highway 24.

There is about three miles of hiking here with your destination a series of self-contained groundwater ponds. Tannins from decaying pine needles leaching into the ponds have darkened the water and also poisoned it for most fish. The origins of these water-filled depressions is unkown; perhaps the remnants of a receding sea or maybe sinkholes. Your dog won't concern herself with that when she needs to cool off, however.

Trail Sense: An interpretive brochure/trail map is available at the trailhead kiosk and the trail is beautifully marked with color-coded signposts at trail junctions.

Carteret

Phone Number
- (252) 393-8185

Website
- www.nccoast.org/

Admission Fee
- None

Park Hours
- Daylight hours

Directions
- *Cape Carteret*; on the north side of Highway 24 east of townand west of Morehead City, across from the North Carolina Coastal Federation office.

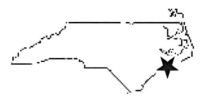

A rare obstacle to the easy canine hiking on the **Patsy Pond Nature Trail.**

Dog Friendliness

Dogs are welcome to hike here.

Traffic

Foot traffic only and not a great deal of that. Hunting is allowed from October to February and April to May.

Canine Swimming

Wait until you get to the beach; when the trails touch on the edges of the ponds access is soft and swampy.

Trail Time

About an hour to circle these tranquil trails.

17
Fort Macon State Park

The Park

The need for the defense of Beaufort Inlet became apparent in the early dawn hours of 1747 when Spanish raiders sacked the town of Beaufort. It took another 50 years for a formal masonry fort to be completed on the tip of Bogue Banks but in 1825 it was washed away by a huricane.

By 1826, behind the efforts of North Carolina Senator Nathaniel Macon, a new fort was underway. In the 1840s the critical task of keeping back the sea was assigned to a young Army engineer named Robert E. Lee.

At the start of the Civil War, North Carolina quickly took control of the fort but the garrison surrendered on April 26, 1862 to Generals John C. Parke and Ambrose Burnside after a land and sea bombardment. For the duration of the war Fort Macon served as a coaling station for Union navy ships.

After the war the seacoast brick fort was a federal prison for a time and was eventually abandoned following the Spanish-American War in 1903. The state purchased the property for one dollar in 1924 and it became North Caolina's second state park.

Carteret

Phone Number
- (252) 726-3775

Website
- http://ils.unc.edu/parkproject/visit/foma/home.html

Admission Fee
- None

Park Hours
- Open at 8:00 a.m. every day; closes at 6:00 p.m. Nov-Feb, 7:00 p.m. Mar and Oct. 8:00 p.m. Apr, May and Sep, 9:00 p.m. Jun-Aug

Directions
- *Atlantic Beach*; two miles east of yown at the end of Route 58.

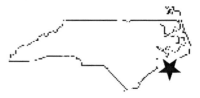

The Walks

Formal hiking at Fort Macon State Park is reserved for the .4-mile *Elliot Coues Nature Trail* that runs through low-lying sand dunes between the Beaufort Inlet and the fort. But this is just an appetizer for your dog in the park.

Your dog is welcome to hike in, around and on top of Fort Macon.

The prime attraction for canine hikers here is the best dune-backed beach walking on the Crystal Coast. In addition to the wide sand at low tide your dog can explore the shallow waters and crannies around the jetty at the end of the island. And when your dog's thoughts turn to cool grass you are welcome to wander among the ramparts of Fort Macon.

Trail Sense: A park map is available but not necessary.

Dog Friendliness
Dogs are allowed throughout the park except in the bathouse or at the swimming area.

Traffic
Swimming is not allowed at the tip of the island so the beach is reserved for walkers.

Canine Swimming
The park is surrounded on three sides by water with plenty of chance for your dog to get a dip.

Trail Time
More than an hour.

18
Audubon Newhall Preserve

The Park

Charles Fraser was the inventor of the modern seaside resort community, gobbling up 5,000 acres of land and towering pine trees on the southern side of Hilton Head Island for his visionary Sea Pines Plantation in 1957. He first envisioned only being able to sell home lots by the seaside but by 1965 it was becoming apparent that the appeal of Sea Pines would be far greater than that.

Realizing the need to save some of the island woodlands Caroline ("Beany") Newhall persuaded Fraser to donate 50 acres of land for the Preserve. She worked tirelessly nurturing native plants and habitats in the protected area and in 1976 Beany Newhall deeded the Preserve to the Hilton Head Island Audubon Society.

The Walks

There are eight small areas of exploration in the Preserve, all centering around a woodland pond. The 12-foot deep depression was excavated in 1965 and restored in 1993. Water temperatures can range from 50 to 90 degrees and over 50 species of plants line the edge, most identified by small label signs.

The hiking is easy for your dog here with soft dirt, pine straw and mulch under paw. The well-groomed paths traverse a patchwork of southern flora from

Beaufort

Phone Number
- None

Website
- None

Admission Fee
- None

Park Hours
- Daylight hours

Directions
- *Hilton Head Island*; from US 278 take the Cross-Island Expressway (toll-road). After passing Palmetto Bay Road turn right at the Preserve sign, just before reaching Sea Pines Plantation.

Florida scrub to native Lowcountry hardwoods. A thick understory of shrubs is dominated by ferns and saw palmetto.

Trail Sense: A detailed trail guide and scrupiously attended signs on the property lead you around.

Audubon Newhall Preserve is typified by a jungle-like understory.

Dog Friendliness

This is the type of park dogs normally are not allowed to enjoy so it is a real treat that dogs can trot these trails.

Traffic

The parking lot is scarcely large enough for a half-dozen cars so you most likely will enjoy solitary explorations of the Preserve with your dog.

Canine Swimming

You don't want to allow your dog in the pond.

Trail Time

More than one hour.

Happiness is dog-shaped.
-Chapman Pincher

19
Awendaw Passage of the Palmetto Trail

The Park

The *Palmetto Trail* was conceived in 1994 to be one of only 13 cross-state trails in America. The target date for completion of the 425 miles of hike-and-bike trail from Mountains to Sea is 2010. The *Awendaw Passage* is the lowcountry eastern anchor for the *Palmetto Trail*.

The Walks

The *Awendaw Passage* jitterbugs for seven miles, most of it on a bluff above the Awendaw Creek. The canine hiking here rises above the typical fare found in long pine corridors with its sweeping vistas of the marsh and Intracoastal Waterway.

The groomed natural surface alternates with wild, untamed stretches, rooty mud and boardwalks. Still, if trail maintenance has had a chance to catch up with the latest storm, this should be easy going for any dog. After crossing US 17 at the 5-mile mark, if the terrain hasn't been flat enough for you, the *Awendaw Passage* utilizes an old railroad grade.

This trail sets up beautifully for a car shuttle but if you are visiting with just one car you will want to go out-and-back from the Buck Hall Recreation Area for full scenic impact.

Charleston

Phone Number
- (843) 336-3248

Website
- http://palmettoconservation.
org/index.php?action=website-
view&WebSiteID=127&WebPag
eID=2452

Admission Fee
- Parking fee for Buck Hall
Recreation Area

Park Hours
- Sunrise to sunset

Directions
- *Awendaw*; the northern trailhead at Buck Hall Recreation
Area is on the east side of US
17, 6.5 miles south of McClellanville and 3 miles north of
Awendaw. Parking at the south
terminus is available at the
Swamp Fox Trailhead on the
west side of US 17 south of
the town of Awendaw.

Some day these will be the first steps for a trail that travels 425 miles across South Carolina on the **Palmetto Trail.**

Trail Sense: Trail guides for the *Palmetto Trail* are so detailed that they include descriptions of turns in the trail. Catching hold of one at the trailhead is more problematic.

Dog Friendliness
Dogs are allowed on the trail and in the campground.
Traffic
The trail is open to foot and bike traffic.
Canine Swimming
Your dog's best chance for a doggie dip is at the boat launch in the Buck Hall Recreation Area.
Trail Time
Several hours out on the trail.

20
Neusiok
Trail

The Park

This region was heavily populated by members of the Algonquian and Iroquoian tribes, whose languages contributed many of the names to eastern North Carolina. Neusiok was the name of a village - just one of many that would be deserted when the coastal Indians were driven from their ancestral lands to northern Pennsylvania and New York.

The 20.4-mile *Neusiok Trail* in the Croatan National Forest is the longest hiking trail in coastal North Carolina. Originally laid out by the Carteret County Wildlife Club in 1971, the *Neusiok Trail* is part of the 900-mile *Mountains-to-Sea Trail* that begins in Great Smoky Mountains National Park and ends in Jockey Ridge State Park at the ocean.

The Walks

Hiking the *Neusiok Trail* from end to end will take you from sandy beaches on the Neuse River to a salt marsh on the Newport River. This is easy going for your dog with just enough elevation change to allow loblolly and longleaf pines to mingle with oaks and hickories. Thanks to active trail maintenance much of the slogging through low-lying areas has been eliminated by wooden walkways.

Craven/Carteret

Phone Number
- (252) 638-5628

Website
- www.cs.unca.edu/nfsnc/recreation/neusiok_trail.pdf

Admission Fee
- None

Park Hours
- Sunrise to sunset

Directions
- *Newport, the southern terminus*; in town, follow Market Street to Mill Creek Road (SR 1154). Go 7.1 miles to Oyster Point Road (FR 181) and turn right for one mile to the campground.

Havelock, the northern terminus; turn onto NC 101 and go 5.3 miles to Ferry Road (NC 306). Turn left on NC 306 and go 3.3 miles to Forest Road 132. Turn left on unpaved road. Go 1.7 miles to Pine Cliff Picnic Area at road's end.

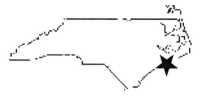

At the southern terminus of the Neusiok Trail at Oyster Point you can indulge in the passion for Carolina's favorite mollusk - the oyster. There is a myth that fat, fleshy oysters can only be enjoyed in months without a "r" in their names but oysters are edible year-round.
In summer, however, oysters are spawning and low in the glycogen that makes them sweet.

The marshy shores of the Newport River are an ideal place for your dog to cool down after a fun day of hiking the Neusiok Trail.

The trail crosses several roads and access points so it is possible to experience the quiet of the national forest in hikeable chunks. For dogs tackling the entire route without transportation arrangements camping is allowed anywhere along the trail and three trail shelters offer refuge.

Trail Sense: The trail is marked in rectangular metal tags so as to survive periodic prescribed burning of the forest.

Dog Friendliness
Dogs are allowed throughout the national forest.

Traffic
Foot traffic only and you can expect to spend hours on the trail in solitude.

Canine Swimming
The best doggie swimming holes are at either end.

Trail Time
A full day and more.

21
ACE Basin National Wildlife Refuge

The Park

Long the domain of rice plantations and hunting retreats, the ACE
Basin represents one of the largest undeveloped wetland ecosystems remaining
on the Atlantic Coast. The centerpiece
of the refuge is the Grove Plantation
that was an original land grant to
Robert Fenwick in 1694. The property
descended through a parade of owners
(one being Owen Winston, a president
of Brooks Brothers) until the U.S. Fish
& Wildlife Service purchased the Grove
Plantation in 1992. Along with another
unit on the Combahee River, the ACE
Basin National Wildlife Refuge encompasses 11,062 acres and is growing.

Charleston

Phone Number
- (843) 889-3084

Website
- http://acebasin.fws.gov

Admission Fee
- None

Hours
- 7:30 a.m. to 4:00 p.m.

Directions
- *Edisto Unit;* from US 17 take
SC 174 towards Edisto Beach.
At a flashing light after Adams
run make a right on Willtown
Road (Route 346). The entrance
road is two miles on the left.

The Walks

For a day of pure hiking with your
dog in solitude come to this refuge along
the South Edisto River. Come with a
mind to explore - these are not groomed
trails.

When you set out, you will never be
sure what you will get. Maybe a rough
dirt path. Maybe an old road. Maybe a

former railroad grade. Maybe a woodland. Maybe old fields. Maybe a cypress
swamp. Maybe a grove of old oaks.

There are miles of roads and walking trails criss-crossing the refuge impoundments that will delight any level of canine hiker.

Trail Sense: A simple trail map is your only navigational friend here.

The Grove Plantation House is one of the last surviving antebellum plantation houses built before the War Bewteen the States still standing in the ACE Basin.

Dog Friendliness
Dogs are welcome in the refuge.
Traffic
Almost none.
Canine Swimming
Keep your dog on land - there are alligators here.
Trail Time
Several hours available.

22
Cedar Point
Recreation Area

The Park

A part of the 161,000 acres of the Croatan National Forest, Cedar Point is in the extreme southwestern corner of the forest at the mouth of the White Oak River. Here, the mixing of salt water and freshwater creates a nutrient-rich nursery where 95% of commercially harvested finfish and shellfish spend some time during their lives.

The Walks

For such a tranquil canine hike this is quite a violent place. Hurricanes and storms routinely flood the freshwater marshes with saltwater that kills some trees and leaves others vulnerable to predacious insects. Death and destruction are so common here visitors are warned of the dangers of collapsing dead trees. Hurricanes Fran and Bertha each took a frightful toll in 1996, especially among the 100-foot loblolly pines that once graced the marsh.

Carteret

Phone Number
- (252) 638-5628

Website
- www.cs.unca.edu/nfsnc/recreation/cedar_point.pdf

Admission Fee
- None

Park Hours
- Sunrise to sunset

Directions
- *Swansboro*; off NC 58 about 1.25 miles north of the junction of NC 24 and NC 58.

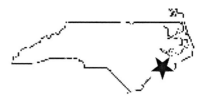

Your dog will be trotting along the hard-pack and boardwalks of the *Tideland Trail*, a designated National Recreation Trail. The loop is 1.3 miles around but if the bugs are too pesky in the summer - and don't forget to spray your dog with insect repellent - there is a cut-off to shorten your trail time. This is easy, level going but you may want to take advantage of the many trailside benches to contemplate your special surroundings.

Trail Sense: A mapboard is available at the trailhead and there is no chance of getting lost on the trail.

Bonus

As you walk one of the eight boardwalks across the marsh you can look down onto the mud flats and observe the herds of fiddler crabs scurrying about, obviously very busy. They are collecting sediment that the crab filters for nutrients. The leftover dirt is deposited in a small ball that can most easily be seen beside a burrow hole. Fiddler crabs are easily recognized by the large, asymmetical claw wielded only by the males. The impressive weapon is waved in the air to impress females and can occasionally be used in open warfare with a rival amorous male. The name "Fiddler Crab" comes from the feeding of the males, where the movement of the small claw from the ground to its mouth resembles the motion of a musician moving a bow across a fiddle.

Dog Friendliness
Dogs can use the trail and stay overnight in the campground.

Traffic
Foot traffic only but little of it.

Canine Swimming
Use the boat ramp for a doggie swim in the White Oak River.

Trail Time
About one hour.

Salt water intrusion dooms many trees at Cedar Point.

23
Santee Coastal Reserve

The Park

Once a vast rice plantation, the Nature Conservancy was given this land in 1974 by the Santee Gun Club. It was eventually turned over to the South Carolina Department of Natural Resources. The result is the 24,000-acre Santee Coastal Reserve.

The Walks

Your first stop in the Santee Coastal Reserve should be the 1.9-mile *Marshland Loop* where your dog will find easy trotting mostly on wide, double-track roads and dikes left over from the rice cultivation days. The highlight of this hike is an 800-foot boardwalk that pierces a freshwater pond speckled with bald cypress and water tupelo, all luxuriously adorned in Spanish moss.

Serious canine hikers may want to depart the *Marshland Loop* for the 6.5-mile trip on the *Bike/Hike Loop* that leads out to the Intracoastal Waterway and South Santee River.

Only serious dog hiking adventurers should consider the 1.1-mile *Woodland Loop* where you are likely to find thick sand, churned up dirt roads and overgrown grass pathways.

Trail Sense: Markings for the *Woodland Trail* are a disaster; things improve down the road at the *Marshland Loop*.

Charleston

Phone Number
- (843) 546-8665

Website
- None

Admission Fee
- None

Park Hours
- Sunrise to sunset

Directions
- *Georgetown;* go 15 miles south (one mile past the South Santee River Bridge) and turn left onto Santee Road. Go 1.4 miles and turn left onto Santee Gun Club Road (gravel road). The parking lot is 3 miles down on the right.

The Washo Reserve features a 200-year-old freshwater cypress lake and cypress-gum swamp, which harbors the oldest wading bird rookery in continuous use in North America. Numerous pairs of osprey nest here, making the Reserve one of the largest concentrations of fish hawks on the east coast. Washo has been named one of America's top 500 Globally Important Bird Areas by the American Bird Conservancy.

Dog Friendliness
Dogs are allowed on the trails in the Santee Coastal Reserve.
Traffic
More bikes than hikers but don't expect much of either.
Canine Swimming
Alligators live here so save the canine aquatics for another day.
Trail Time
Many hours of canine hiking are possible.

This majestic oak on the Woodland Trail is typical of the lush forestation to be found by your dog at the Santee Coastal Reserve.

24
Currituck National Wildlife Refuge

The Park

The Migratory Bird Conservation Committee established Currituck National Wildlife Refuge on August 2, 1983 to protect a portion of the Outer Banks favored by wintering waterfowl and other migratory birds. The refuge covers 4,103 acres across sandy beaches, grassy dunes, maritime forests, shrub thickets, and fresh and brackish marshes.

The Walks

Currituck Refuge does not have any developed public use facilities such as roads, trails, restrooms, or visitor contact station. Just pull in, get out with your dog and start exploring. This would be much like the first Europeans would have found when they began arriving in the late 1500s.

A diverse population of wildlife congregate here. One species you might see are the Corolla Wild Horses that have wandered off their Wild Horse Sanctuary. You may exult in seeing the ponies but the U.S. Fish and Wildlife Service considers them a non-native nuisance animal competing with the protected species for food and actively work to minimze their impact.

Trail Sense: There is nothing to map - you will only bring a dog with an explorer's heart to Currituck Refuge.

Currituck

Phone Number
- (252) 429-3100

Website
- www.fws.gov/mackayisland/currituck/

Admission Fee
- None

Park Hours
- One half-hour before sunrise to one half-hour after sunset

Directions
- *Corolla*; the Refuge is located 3/4 of a mile north of town. NC 12 ends in Corolla; after the road ends proceed up the beach 3/4 of a mile to the first Refuge tract.

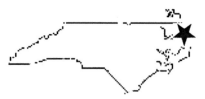

The sun greets another dog day over Currituck National Wildlife Refuge.

Dog Friendliness
Dogs are permitted in the Refuge.

Traffic
The Refuge averages about 50 visitors a day and many times during the year you and your dog may be the only ones here.

Canine Swimming
Yes, the Atlantic Ocean.

Trail Time
More than one hour.

25
South Tibwin Hiking Trail

The Park

The Francis Marion National Forest was established in 1936, protecting some 600,000 acres of trees in South Carolina. The South Tibwin tract was a rice plantation established in 1803 on the salt marshes along the Atlantic Ocean. Much of the impoundments on the property are the handiwork of slaves from that early 19th century heyday.

The Walks

Canine hiking here is a rustic affair on flat hardwood bottomlands with a preponderance of pine trees near the highway. Park just after pulling off US 17 and walk your dog through the gate into the maze of old roads and cart paths. Off the main road you will often encounter natural double-track paths, some heavily sheathed in grass. It can be a messy affair in times of wet weather.

The primitive trail system covers about five miles, mostly leading to three freshwater ponds on the property. These ponds will just be looking for your dog - they do contain alligators. Almost all your dog's steps here will be shaded by forest.

Trail Sense: There is a trail map to take along but the trails are not marked.

Charleston

Phone Number
- (843) 887-3257

Website
- www.fs.fed.us/r8/fms/

Admission Fee
- None

Hours
- Sunrise to sunset

Directions
- *Awendaw;* on the east side of US 17, 2.3 miles south of McClellanville and 12.5 miles north of the Sewee Visitor and Environmental Education Center in Awendaw.

Dog Friendliness

Dogs are permitted and can go under voice control in the Francis Marion National Forest.

Traffic

Bikes are allowed but sightings of other trail users on the South Tibwin trail system will be infrequent. No motor vehicles allowed.

Canine Swimming

Keep your dog out of the ponds - alligators live here.

Trail Time

More than one hour.

26
Fort Raleigh
National Historic Site

The Park

England came late to the game of colonization in the New World. The Spanish were already entrenched in Florida and Mexico for sixty years before Sir Humphrey Gilbert sailed to Newfoundland with the first English settlement parties. His efforts failed and he died in the effort but his half-brother Sir Walter Raleigh picked up his flagging venture.

The next wave of English came in 1585 on seven ships commanded by Raleigh's cousin, Sir Richard Grenville. A party of 108 colonists was left on Roanoke Island, which they considered "a most pleasant and fertile ground."

When supply ships returned in 1587 there was no trace of "The Cittie of Ralegh." Attempts to locate the colonists were made until 1602 but they had disappeared without a trace. Maybe they were killed by local Indian tribes, maybe there were too many mercantile and scientific types in the colony and not enough tradesmen and farmers. To this day no one knows the true fate of the Lost Colony.

Dare
Phone Number - (252) 473-5772
Website - www.nps.gov/fora/
Admission Fee - None
Hours - Sunrise to sunset
Directions - *Manteo;* 3 miles north of town on US 64 on Roanoke Island.

The Walks

The canine hiking here is along the superior *Thomas Hariot Nature Trail*. Hariot was a 25-year old astronomer and mathematician chosen as observer and chronicler for the initial voyage. He taught himself Algonquian and served as liaison between the colonists and the local Indians.

The well-groomed loop dips and rolls after starting out from the reconstructed fort. This hike is completely shaded and points out things the colonists could have done to survive on interpretive signs. It also includes quotes from Hariot's notebooks. The route touches on Roanoke Sound where your dog can find a small sand beach and excellent dog paddling.

Trail Sense: The trail is well-marked and a park brochure available.

Dog Friendliness
Dogs are allowed on the grounds at Fort Raleigh.

Traffic
Foot traffic only and more folks are interested in watching the dramatization of *The Lost Colony* in the park theater than exploring it.

Canine Swimming
Yes, in Roanoke Sound.

Trail Time
About one hour.

If there are no dogs in Heaven,
then when I die I want to go where they went.
-Anonymous

27
Fort Moultrie

The Park

In January 1776 Charlestonians began to defend their town by starting construction of a fort on Sullivan's Island. Six months later the palmetto log-and-sand fortification showed only two walls facing the harbor and two incomplete walls exposed to Long Island to the rear. Meanwhile British amphibious forces were massing offshore.

Rather than sail by the meager American defenses into Charleston Sir Henry Clinton chose to destroy the unnamed fort. Nine powerful warships opened fire on the morning of June 28. The crude fort proved to be an ideal bastion, as the spongy palmetto wood received the cannon balls without splintering. The sand mortar absorbed what the palmetto could not. After nine hours the British fleet and its more than 200 guns was forced to retire. Charleston would remain unmolested for three more years.

The little fort was subsequently-named for its commander, William Moultrie. After the Revolution Fort Moultrie was neglected, and by 1791 little remained. Under a nationwide system of seacoast fortifications, Fort Moultrie was rebuilt in 1798 and remained active until World War II. The fort stands today under the administration of the National Park Service as a unit of the Fort Sumter National Monument.

Charleston

Phone Number
- (843) 883-3123

Website
- www.nps.gov/fosu/

Admission Fee
- Yes, for the fort where dogs are not allowed

Park Hours
- Sunrise to sunset

Directions
- *Sullivan's Island*; from US 17 take SC 703 to Sullivan's Island. Cross the Intracoastal Waterway at the Ben Sawyer Bridge and continue straight on Ben Sawyer Boulevard to Middle Street. Turn right and go 1.5 miles to the Visitor Center.

The Walks

The maze of sand-and-grass paths that wander around Fort Moultrie and Battery Jasper make for an easy open-air exploration for your dog. The real hiking comes when you split a small dune and arrive on the beach at Sullivan's Island. Here your dog can go off-leash much of the year and a couple of miles of sandy beach await. Fort Sumter,

The **Cannon Walk** *stirs the echoes of Fort Moultrie through the decades.*

where the first shots of the Civil War rang out, is clearly seen in Charleston Harbor from the beach.

Trail Sense: Everything is pretty much laid out in front of you.

Dog Friendliness

Dogs are welcome on the grounds but not inside the fort and not on the ferry to Fort Sumter or at Fort Sumter if arriving by private boat.

Traffic

If you are coming to lay a blanket on the beach around Charleston, this probably won't be your destination so it's a wonderful place to bring your beach-loving dog.

Canine Swimming

Bring your dog's swimming trunks when you come to Fort Moultrie.

Trail Time

More than one hour.

28
Wannamaker County Park

The Park

Wannamaker Park opened in 1998 - a spacious park sprawling across more than 1000 acres, about evenly split between dry highlands and beautiful cypress wetlands. Although designed to serve the usual recreation needs of a suburban populace the park retains much of its natural feel.

The Walks

Your dog will find plenty of trail time here with two miles of paved multi-use paths and another two miles of nature trails. The park has been designed so the trails lead away from the recreational areas so don't get discouraged if you are sitting in a line with hundreds of kids at the entrance gate - they are probably headed for the water park and play hill.

The central loop swings around a five-acre lagoon while a more private loop skips out towards the Goose Creek Reservoir. There is plenty of shade on these trails and easy canine hiking afoot. When your hike is done an expansive grass meadow is begging for a spirited game of fetch.

Trail Sense: A park map is available to plan your dog's outing in Wannamaker Park.

Charleston

Phone Number
- (843) 795-4386

Website
- http://ccprc.com/index.asp?nid=70

Admission Fee
- $1.00

Park Hours
- Open 8:00 a.m. every day; closes 5:00 p.m. Nov-Feb, 6:00 p.m. Mar and Oct, 7:00 p.m. Apr and Sep, 8:00 p.m. May-Aug

Directions
- *North Charleston*; at the intersection of Routes 78 and 52. The main entrance is at 8888 University Boulevard (Route 78).

Dog Friendliness

Dogs are allowed on the park trails.

Traffic

This is a popular park but the trails are probably the least-used feature.

Canine Swimming

Water sports for dogs are not the prime attraction at Wannamaker Park.

Trail Time

More than one hour.

29
Mackay Island National Wildlife Refuge

The Park

Over the years the name Mackay Island has been corrupted from John Mackie, who purchased "Orphan's Island in 1761. Several famous owners filtered through the years, including Thomas Dixon, author of *The Birth of a Nation*.

Dixon sold the island to New York publishing baron Joseph P. Knapp who created the first Sunday newspaper supplement in America. Knapp built a resort here and began adapting innovative wildlife management techniques to the marshes that dominate the island.

Knapp would go on to found the influential conservation group Ducks Unlimited, holding the first organizational meeting in 1936. After his death in 1951 logging began on the island before the U.S. Fish & Wildlife Service acquired the island in 1960.

Currituck

Phone Number
- (252) 429-3100

Website
- www.mackayisland.fws.gov

Admission Fee
- None

Park Hours
- Daylight hours

Directions
- *Knotts Island*; accessible via free ferry from Currituck. The entrance to the Refuge is on the left along Route 615, about four miles north of the ferry landing.

The Walks

The Refuge covers more than 8,000 acres, about 75% of which is brackish marshes. You can take your dog on long, quiet hikes along roads that loop around the impoundments. These flat dirt roads lead out to Currituck Sound and back and the biggest loop - the *Live Oak Point Trail* - will cover almost six miles. Most of this canine hiking is out in the open with little shade and much of the Refuge is closed during the cooler months (mid-October to mid-March for wintering migrations) so bring plenty of drinking water before setting out.

Shorter routes, the *Great Marsh Loop Trail* and the *Marsh Causeway*, are both open year-round. The *Great Marsh Loop* is a true hiking trail, less than a half-mile, that starts beside a fishing hole and sweeps through swamp-like terrain.

Trail Sense: A park brochure is available from kiosks at Refuge entrances.

Dog Friendliness
Dogs are allowed on all the roads and trails.

Traffic
You will be sharing the Mackay Island roads with the very occasional vehicle or cyclist.

Canine Swimming
There is plenty of water around although hiking is your main attraction in the refuge.

Trail Time
Several hours of trail time are available.

It's the wide open spaces for your dog on the lightly traveled roads of the Mackay Island National Wildlife Refuge.

30
Moores Creek National Battlefield

The Park

In the years before the American Revolution a steady stream of Scottish Highlanders populated the North Carolina interior and on February 20, 1776 General Donald MacDonald organized some 1,600 Loyalists to march to the sea and join the regular British Army.

The march could funnel across Moores Creek - a dark, sluggish stream - at only one place and alerted American volunteers hastily erected earthworks on the other side. The Americans had the superior position but a British scout reported only a camp on the west side of the creek - not the fortifications on the east side.

The camp was a decoy and the Tories marched into a trap. Planks on the Moores Creek bridge were removed and the Highlanders had to pick their way through the fog across the creek. Reach-

Pender

Phone Number
- (910) 283-5591

Website
- www.nps.gov/mocr/

Admission Fee
- None

Park Hours
- 9:00 a.m. to 5:00 p.m.

Directions
- *Currie*; just west of town on Route 210. About 20 miles northwest of Wilmington, reached by I-40 or US 421.

ing the opposite bank they were met with withering fire at the earthworks. What Patriot musketry didn't take care of, a swivel gun and artillery did. The Loyalists lost 30 killed and 40 wounded. Only one Patriot died.

The victory demonstrated surprising Patriot strength, discouraging the growth of Loyalist sentiment in the Carolinas and convincing the British there would be no quick crushing of the rebellion. In fact, a little more than one month later North Carolina instructed its delegation to the Continental Congress in Philadelphia to vote for independence, the first American colony to do so. Big consequences emanated from a small battle in the swamps of North Carolina.

The Walks

Moores Creek is a winning combination of park and historical site. The one-mile interpretive history trail rolls across a well-groomed landscape of pine trees, open space and a winding creek. The reconstructed bridge and preserved earthworks, rehabilitated in the 1930s, vividly tell the tale of the trap set by the Patriots and the unwelcome terrain the Loyalist had to fight through.

There is more convivial canine hiking around the picnic area and on the *Tarheel Trail*. This interpretive path ducks into the forests to interpret the production of naval stores (tar, pitch and tupentine) that were the region's chief economic resource during the Revolution.

Trail Sense: A detailed park map and brochure is available.

Dog Friendliness
Dogs are allowed throughout the park.
Traffic
Foot traffic only and little of it.
Canine Swimming
There is no good access to Moores Creek.
Trail Time
About one hour.

31
Bird Island
Coastal Reserve

The Park

Bird Island became North Carolina's tenth Coastal Reserve in 2002 after an appropriation of $4.2 million to save the unspoiled barrier island from development. Bird Island preserves 1200 acres of dunes, salt marshes and maritime forests.

The Walks

When Mad Inlet silted up in the 1990s it became possible to walk directly onto Bird Island from Sunset Beach. And doing so is one of the best beach hikes you can take with your dog on the Carolina coasts.

Bird Island is about one mile long with a half-mile expanse of pristine sandy white beach backed by high natural dunes and acres of exquisite salt marsh and meandering tidal creeks. The island is home to a wide variety of plants and animals and it provides habitat for nesting loggerhead sea turtles and waterbirds.

This is all beach-walking for your dog with no shade whatsoever so plan accordingly.

Trail Sense: None, just up and down the beach.

Brunswick

Phone Number
- None

Website
- www.ncnerr.org/pubsiteinfo/ siteinfo/Bird_Island/bird_is- land.html

Admission Fee
- None

Park Hours
- Sunrise to sunset

Directions
- *Sunset Beach*; the Reserve begins at the west end of town, beyond the end of 40th Street. Take US 17 South to NC 904. Turn left. Take 904 to NC 179. Turn right. Take 179 across the Sunset Beach Bridge. Cross the causeway onto Sunset Beach and turn right on the first street, which is North Shore Drive. Drive until you dead end at 40th Street.

There goes the sun, disappearing over Bird Island Coastal Reserve.

Dog Friendliness
Dogs are allowed year-round except 8:00 a.m. to 6:00 p.m. Memorial Day to Labor Day.
Traffic
Foot traffic only; picks up towards sunset down the beach but parking is limited in Sunset Beach.
Canine Swimming
Yes, the Atlantic Ocean.
Trail Time
More than one hour.

32
Alligator River National Wildlife Refuge

The Park

Alligator River National Wildlife Refuge was established on March 14, 1984 to protect a unique wetland habitat type - the pocosin between the Alligator River and the Croatan Sound. The Refuge covers more than 150,000 acres, stretching 28 miles from north to south and 15 miles from east to west.

The intermingling of fresh and brackish water supports a rich cornucopia of plant and animal life. The Refuge is one of the last remaining strongholds for the black bear in eastern North Carolina.

The Walks

Like most wildlife refuges the bulk of your hiking with your dog will be on unpaved, lightly used park roads. Some are closed to all motorized vehicles, others not. All the canine hiking here is flat and easy.

Dare/Hyde
Phone Number - (252) 473-1131
Website - www.fws.gov/alligatorriver
Admission Fee - None
Park Hours - Daylight hours
Directions - *Manteo*; take US 64 west from town, cross the Croatan Sound onto mainland Dare County, and continue west to the Refuge entrance.

There are two short wildlife trails at Alligator River, both about half-mile strips - neither loops. The destination for the paved *Creef Cut Wildlife Trail* is a boardwalk over a freshwater marsh. Look for black bear here. The *Sandy Ridge Wildlife Trail* beats an earthen path to an extensive boardwalk through a cypress swamp. Look for alligators here.

The best trails for your dog in the Refuge are on the water, not the land - bring a canoe. There are more than a dozen miles of paddling trails along the Milltail Creek, including a 1.5-mile loop.

Trail Sense: A park map shows the Refuge roads and there is information at trailhead kiosks.

The red wolf, slightly smaller cousin to the more familiar gray wolf, is one of the most endangered animals on the planet. By 1970, the entire population of red wolves was esimated to be fewer than 100 roaming a small area of swampland in Texas and Louisiana. The U.S. Fish and Wildlife Service captured as many as possible and began a breeding program. Just 14 animals stood between existence and extinction for the red wolf. Since 1987, red wolves have been released into northeastern North Carolina's wildlife refuges. The Refuge is ground zero for the re-introduction and in 1988 the first litter of red wolf pups was born in the wild here. Their numbers in the wild have now increased to around 100.

You would need to be awfully lucky to spot one but if you do a red wolf will be about the size of a German Shepherd with mostly brown and buff coloring and sometimes a reddish tint behind the ears, on the muzzle and on the back of the legs.

Dog Friendliness

Dogs are permitted in the Refuge.

Traffic

An occasional vehicle, an occasional cyclist, a very occasional hiker.

Canine Swimming

At the boat ramps in East Lake, the Alligator River and Stumpy Point Bay.

Trail Time

More than one hour.

33
Currituck Heritage Park

The Park

The name Currituck comes down from the Algonquian Indian term for "Land of the Wild Goose." And it was the abundance of waterfowl that led Edward C. Knight Jr., an heir to an old money Philadelphia fortune, to come here and indulge his passion for bird hunting in the 1920s.

Knight and his wife Marie Louise, built the largest and most elegant residence ever to grace the Outer Banks. Designed in the Beaux Arts style the Knights sunk $400,000 in 1925 into their three-story home with a copper roofline and five brick chimneys. The house featured cork floors, Tiffany light fixtures and hot and cold, fresh and salt water baths. The full basement, swimming pool and elevator were all the first ever seen on the Outer Banks. The Knights called their estate Corolla Island.

After the Knights died their home was sold for $25,000 to Ray Adams. Renamed the Whalehead Club, it fell into disrepair over the decades. In October 1992, the Whalehead Club, listed on the National Register of Historic Places, and 28.5 acres of land were purchased by Currituck County for this park. The Knight home has been restored to its original splendor and is now open for tours.

Currituck

Phone Number
- (252) 453-9040

Website
- www.whaleheadclub.com

Admission Fee
- None

Park Hours
- Sunrise to sunset

Directions
- *Corolla;* on the Outer Banks. After crossing the Wright Memorial Bridge on NC 158 continue to Route 12. Go left and head 20 miles north to the park on the left.

The Walks

Does your dog find herself missing green grass after too much time at the beach? Then this is the place to come. The park doesn't maintain formal hiking trails but there is plenty of room to roam the grounds. The green grass is spotted with live oaks and fingers of grass reach into the Currituck Sound in several locations.

Of course, while you're here you may as well go to the beach as well. Across the road from Currituck Heritage Park is easy access to miles of undisturbed beach. *USA Today* has named Corolla Beach as one of ten best beaches in America.

Trail Sense: You are on your own to poke around with your dog and discover the Whalehead Club.

Dog Friendliness

Dogs are welcome in Currituck Heritage Park.

Traffic

Relaxation and not hustle and bustle are the watchwords for the park.

Canine Swimming

Your dog can sample the gentle waters of Currituck Sound or go across the street and enjoy the Atlantic Ocean.

Trail Time

About an hour in the park.

The Whalehead Club and Corolla Beach are places for your dog to relax and play.

85

34
Hugh MacRae Park

The Park

The MacRae family emigrated from Kintail, Scotland to Wilmington around 1770. Four generations later Hugh MacRae, then only 24 years old, purchased 16,000 acres of land, including Grandfather and Grandmother Mountains, to develop as tourist havens.

By the end of the 19th century, MacRae had become president of his father's company, Wilmington Cotton Mills, and the Wilmington Gas Light Company. Later, he founded Hugh MacRae & Co. in 1902 to develop Wrightsville Beach, Winter Park, and others.

In 1925 MacRae donated land for the Wilmington park to the residents of New Hanover County. Hugh MacRae Park was dedicated as the first county park in May 1954.

New Hanover

Phone Number
- None

Website
- None

Admission Fee
- None

Park Hours
- Sunrise to sunset and early evenings

Directions
- *Wilmington;* downtown at the northeast corner of Oleander Drive and College Avenue (Route 132). The entrance is on College Avenue.

The Walks

Looking for a place to walk the dog in downtown Wilmington? This is the place to come. Widely spaced pine trees anchor attractive plantings around a centerpiece sunken pond that has been cleared out in recent years. An aerating fountain adds beauty and keeps the water clear.

The park is criss-crossed with natural-surface walking paths so your route with your dog is never predetermined. One place that will be on the agenda every visit is the unfenced off-leash area that is marked off by red posts. You can find it across from the pond towards the back-middle of the park.

The scenic pond at Hugh MacRae Park is popular with wedding parties - and dogs.

If you are looking for a more traditional urban recreation hike with your dog head south on College Avenue and turn right on 17th Street to Halyburton Memorial Park at 4099 17th Street. Here you'll find a 1.5-mile multi-use trail around the perimeter of this 58-acre park.

Trail Sense: None; come to poke around with your dog.

Dog Friendliness
Dogs are allowed and poop bags provided.

Traffic
This a good place to come for a communal dog walk.

Canine Swimming
Not here, the ornamental pond is for taking pictures not taking doggie swims.

Trail Time
As much or as little as your dog desires on the honeycomb of paths - and they are lit for night walking.

35
Wright Brothers National Memorial

The Park

Early in the 20th century two Dayton, Ohio bicycle mechanics tamed the skies for all humankind at Kitty Hawk. Orville and Wilbur Wright were lured to the Outer Banks - then a near wilderness - to test their experimental fliers by the high dunes, blustery winds and the promise of soft, sandy landings.

The brothers achieved lift-off and powered flight on December 17, 1903. The first flight lasted only 12 seconds but three subsequent flights that day improved their success exponentially.

The secretive nature of the brothers kept their achievement from becoming public knowledge for several years when improved flyers were demonstrated for huge crowds in New York and Paris.

The Art Deco-influenced stone memorial to the conquest of the air on Big Kill Devil Hill was designed by the architectural firm of Rodgers and Poor and dedicated in 1932.

The Walks

The park features a large open area with two walking destinations of interest. Big Kill Devil Hill, where the Wrights conducted glider tests to test their theories of flight, has been stabilized and is laced with paths around and

Dare

Phone Number
- (252) 473-2111

Website
- www.nps.gov/wrbr/

Admission Fee
- Yes, per vehicle

Hours
- 9:00 a.m. to 5:00 p.m. and 6:00 p.m. during the summer

Directions
- *Kill Devil Hills;* on the Outer Banks at Milepost 7.5 on Route 158.

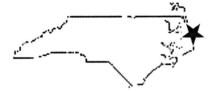

Your dog can hike along the path of the world's first powered flight.

to the top of the 90-foot dune.

Out on the flats you can hike with your dog on rubber mats along the path of the world's first flight. Although it may be tempting to take your dog around the inviting open space, sand spurs and prickly pear are waiting to stab your dog's paws.

Trail Sense: After consulting the park brochure, everything is laid out in front of you.

Dog Friendliness
Dogs are welcome to use the grounds but cannot go in the exhibit buildings.

Traffic
Foot traffic only; bicycles can use the roads with you but cannot go on the walking paths.

Canine Swimming
None.

Trail Time
About one hour.

36
James Island County Park

The Park

Located on the south side of Charleston Harbor, the first cotton mill in South Carolina was built on James Island in 1789. This 643-acre park, not far from downtown Charleston, is administered by Charleston County.

The Walks

All the canine hiking in the park is conducted on paved asphalt paths but as far as the genre goes, it is some of the best your dog will find on the hard surface. Three loops, each about a mile-and-a-half, visit meadows and marshes and mix open-air and shady trees for your dog. All the trotting in James Island County Park is flat and easy.

But once your dog eyes the off-leash dog park in the center of the park it might be hard keeping her on the hike. Again, one of the best of its ilk, the unfenced area is on a round peninsula in the lake that offers superb access to canine aquatics with a smooth bank into the water.

Trail Sense: A park map printout is available to help navigate around the paved trails.

Charleston

Phone Number
- (843) 795-4386

Website
- www.ccprc.com/index.asp?nid=68

Admission Fee
- $1.00

Park Hours
- Open 8:00 a.m. every day; closes 5:00 p.m. Nov-Feb, 6:00 p.m. Mar and Oct, 7:00 p.m. Apr and Sep, 8:00 p.m. May-Aug

Directions
- *Charleston*; exit US 17 on the south side of the Ashley River onto Folly Road Boulevard (Route 171). Turn right onto Maybank Highway and left onto Riverland Drive, following brown signs. The park is on the right at 871 Riverland.

Dog Friendliness
Dogs are allowed throughout the park and in the campground.
Traffic
This is a busy park and the multi-use trails are suitable for bikes, strollers and rollerbladers.
Canine Swimming
The lake and its off-leash area are a perfect place to bring your water-loving dog.
Trail Time
More than one hour.

37
Dismal Swamp Canal Trail

The Park

Colonel William Byrd II led a band of surveyors into the swamp in 1728 and the yellow flies, chiggers and ticks he encountered so discouraged him that he described the place as "a vast body of dirt and nastiness." He called it "Dismal" and the name stuck.

George Washington led investors here in 1764 to investigate the building of a canal to extricate timber from the swamp. It wasn't until 1793, however, that slave labor began digging out the waterway between the Elizabeth River in Virginia and the Pasquotank River in North Carolina.

The first flat-bottomed barges went down the 22-mile canal in 1805 and today it is the oldest continually operating canal in the United States. It is recognized as a National Civil Engineering Landmark and is listed on the National Register of Historic Places.

The *Dismal Swamp Canal Trail* opened in July 2005 for hiking, biking, birding and photography.

Camden

Phone Number
- (252) 771-8333

Website
- www.DismalSwamp.com

Admission Fee
- None

Park Hours
- Daylight hours

Directions
- *South Mills*; the Dismal Swamp Canal Welcome Center is three miles south of the Virginia/North Carolina state line on US 17.

The Walks

The *Dismal Swamp Canal Trail* is 4.5 miles long but the heart for most canine hikers is an attractive stretch that hugs the canal for about three miles. The trail is hard-packed under paw and a roomy ten feet wide, usually with an adequate shoulder. Your dog will be trotting through a leafy forest most of the time along the route.

Adjacent to Dismal Swamp Canal Welcome Center you can find a short nature trail that meanders beside the canal and highlights native forest trees. A pedestrian swing bridge leads across the canal and the Dismal Swamp State Natural Area.

Trail Sense: The Welcome Center, North Carolina's first built off an interstate, will provide orientation materials.

Dog Friendliness
Dogs are allowed to use the *Dismal Swamp Canal Trail*.

Traffic
You will be sharing the trail with bicycles and rollerbladers and strollers; no motorized vehicles.

Canine Swimming
The canal area is not developed for swimming access.

Trail Time
Several hours of trail time are available.

38
Pocosin Lakes National Wildlife Refuge

The Park

The Refuge began as a modest conservation area around Pungo Lake in 1963. In 1989 a donation of 93,000 acres from The Conservation Fund led to the creation of the sprawling Pocosin Lakes National Wildlife Refuge. The name comes down from the Algonquian Indian word meaning "swamp on a hill." A bit of a misnomer - there are no hills but the land is slightly elevated compared to the overwhelming flatness of its surroundings.

The area is distinctive for its poor natural drainage which makes it one of the few areas left in the country to naturally create organic rich peat. It takes 100 years to create one inch of peat soil. Historically the lands have been ditched and drained for farming and mining of the peat soils.

Tyrell/Washington

Phone Number
- (252) 796-3004

Website
- http://pocosinlakes.fws.gov

Admission Fee
- None

Park Hours
- Sunrise to sunset

Directions
- *Columbia*; park headquarters and the Walter B. Jones Sr. Center for the Sounds is immediately south of Route 64 in town. Access to the Refuge is along Route 94 South.

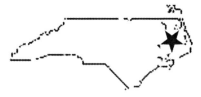

The Walks

Canine hiking in the Refuge is along miles of dirt roads. During periods of wet weather these roads can get quite muddy and during hot weather your dog will be exposed most of the time. But find a cool dry day and this is the place for long, quiet hikes with your dog.

The Refuge touches on five major bodies of water and there is ample opportunities for viewing some of the 200 species of birds that visit Pocosin Lakes. The Refuge is also home to more than 40 species of mammals, including a large population of black bears. At the Walter B. Jones, Sr. Center you can take your dog along the Scuppernong River Interpretive Boardwalk to explore the

wetlands nourished by the waterway.

Adjacent to Pocopsin Lakes, along the Alligator River, is the Emily & Richardson Preyer Buckridge Preserve, another 27,000 acres of protected wetlands. There are no public facilities in this remote site and again canine hiking is conducted along existing roads.

Trail Sense: A park map/brochure points out the roads that can be used for hiking.

Dog Friendliness
  Dogs are permitted to hike the Refuge.
Traffic
  Even the roads that are open to motor vehicles are lightly used.
Canine Swimming
  There are alligators present in the Preserve.
Trail Time
  More than an hour.

39
Emerald Isle Woods Park

The Park

The price of parks has certainly gone up. One of the Carolina coasts' newest parks, the cost of land for this Town of Emerald Isle facility cost $3.28 million for 43 acres in 2002. The park is part of a storm water management program and has been dressed up with hiking trails. Emerald Isle Woods was formally dedicated in July 2006.

The Walks

The main reason you will want to bring your dog to Emerald Isle Woods are for the sporty hills you won't typically find along seashore trails. The first thing you need to know here is to ignore the first trailhead you encounter when you drive down the entrance road. It looks wide and inviting but the trail goes nowhere.

A pastiche of short trails connect the parking lot, the fishing pier and the bathrooms in a triangular pattern. You may have to backtrack during your dog's outing in Emerald Isle Woods but no one should mind on the soft, sandy paths.

Carteret
Phone Number - None **Website** - None **Admission Fee** - None **Park Hours** - Sunrise to sunset **Directions** - *Emerald Isle;* cross the B. Cameron Langston Bridge on NC 58 onto Emerald Isle. Make the first right onto Coast Guard Road and go a 1/2 mile to the park on the right.

If you do stop to sample these trails you will also want to take your dog to the public beach access in Emerald Isle, less than one mile away (make the first right after you pull back onto NC 58 leaving the park.) Dogs are allowed year-round on the white sand beach, with plenty of hiking to be had.

Trail Sense: There are signs pointing out destinations at trail junctions but no map to tell you whether said destination is five minutes or five hours away. It won't take long however to explore the whole park.

Dog Friendliness

Dogs are allowed to use these trails.

Traffic

Foot traffic only and usually not much of it.

Canine Swimming

The Emerald Isle town beach a short distance away is as good as it gets. The access to Bogue Sound is restricted to a pier.

Trail Time

Less than one hour.

Your dog will know Emerald Isle Woods is a new park - check out this bridge!

40
West Ashley Greenway

The Park

West Ashley was the site of the original founding of Charles Town in 1670 and this area is Charleston's oldest suburb. The *West Ashley Greenway* uses an abandoned railroad line to travel out 10.5 miles to John's Island.

The Walks

Unlike most rail-to-trail projects this pathway has not been paved. The hard-packed corridor is bumpy and occasionally pockmarked so canine hikers won't have to deal with road bikes as they do on most rail trails. More typical of other rail trails, there are virtually no hills.

The first three miles or so traverses residential neighborhoods and there are a number of street crossings. Further west the scenery turns rural and marshy. The Clemson Agricultural Experiment Station is here. So if you are just sampling the Greenway this is the end to concentrate your explorations with your dog.

Trail Sense: No maps and you have to look closely for trailheads.

Charleston

Phone Number
- (843) 724-7321

Website
- www.sctrails.net/Trails/ALL-TRAILS/Railtrails/WestAshGreenway.html

Admission Fee
- None

Park Hours
- Sunrise to sunset

Directions
- *Charleston;* cross the Ashley River on US 17 and turn left on Folly Road (Route 171). At the second light turn right into Windermere Shopping Center. The trail is behind the strip center on the right.

Dog Friendliness

Dogs are allowed to hike down the *Greenway*.

Traffic

This is a popular recreation destination for local hikers and mountain bikers.

Canine Swimming

No.

Trail Time

As much or as little as your dog wants.

41
Flanners Beach Trail
Carteret County, North Carolina

Seven miles north of Havelock off US 70 to FSR 1107 to the Neuse River

The Neuse River Campground, known locally as Flanners Beach, is operated by the Croatan National Forest. Nestled on a bluff among tall loblolly pines, the big attraction for dogs here is a long, sandy swimming beach that slopes gently towards the river.

A paved multi-use trails circles the 42-site campground and another serpentine trail explores the pines and hardwoods and cypress swamps for about two miles. This trail has enough undulations to pique the interest of mountain bikers but you will often be at one with your dog here.

42
Fort Lamar Heritage Preserve
Charleston County, South Carolina

On James Island; off SC 171 turn left onto Grimball Road and right on Secessionville Road and left onto Fort Lamar Road

Anytime an army wants to invade Charleston, James Island is a logical point of attack. It happened when the British eyed the town during the Revolution and again in the Civil War. The Confederates began erecting defenses on the island in January 1862 but they were little more than earthworks protected by the muck of tidal marshes.

The battle for the control of James Island began in the pre-dawn hours of June 16, 1862. More than 3500 Union troops stormed the earthen mounds and quickly breached the walls. But the assault was repulsed in heavy hand-to-hand fighting and a second wave of Federals was foiled by the impassable marshes.

The battery would not be finished until 1864 and was named for the 1st South Carolina Artillery commander Colonel Thomas G. Lamar. After his standout performance on James Island, Lamar died of malaria late in 1862. The interpretive trail winds through the earthen magazines that stand across the road from the parking area. The historic Fort Lamar is lightly visited and the area is a bit unkempt but a good place for your dog to romp for a half-hour or so.

43
Charles Pinckney National Historic Site
Charleston County, South Carolina

Just west of US 17 in Mount Pleasant; turn onto Long Point Road north of the intersection with Route 517 to the site on the left

Charles Pinckney began a career of public service at the age of 21 during the American Revolution. Captured by the British in Charleston in 1780 with his father, the elder Pinckney was forced to swear allegiance to the British Crown to save the family estate, Snee Farm, from confiscation.

Charles Pinckney signed the United States Constitution in 1788 and went on to be a four-time governor of South Carolina, a U.S. Senator and Ambassador to Spain. He tried to retire in 1818 but was elected to the United States Congress. The Snee Farm had been sold out of the family by this time although it remained a working plantation for another 100 years.

The original 715-acre Pinckney estate was systematically sold off for houses and a golf course. In 1990, a local preservation group deeded the final 28 undeveloped acres to the National Park Service to create a memorial for one of South Carolina's most influential early legislators.

A short nature trail leads from the plantation house through native red cedars into a typical Southern forest bounding a tidal wetland. This is easy hikng for your dog who is most welcome here - you are enouraged in park publications to "Bring the Dog!"

This small model of a rice trunk demonstrates how rice grew on Snee Farm.

44
The Penn Nature Center
Beaufort County, South Carolina

East of Beaufort on St. Helena Island; turn right on Martin Luther King, Jr.
Drive off US 21 to the Penn Center on the right

The Penn Center was started in 1862 after the Emancipation Proclomation as one of the first schools for newly freed Southern slaves. The first principals were Northern missionaries Laura Towne and Ellen Murray. Both spent the next forty years of their lives living among and educating former Sea Island slaves. The complex of nineteen surviving buildings has been placed on the National Register of Historic Places.

If you are making the drive down US 21 to Hunting Island State Park this   is an ideal break to stop and give your dog a leg stretcher. The one-mile interpretive trail loops along a sandy path past several campus buildings and a garden. Many of the lowcountry's signature hardwood trees are on display along the way: live oaks draped in Spanish moss, black walnuts, pecans and magnolias among them.

Your dog is welcome on the grounds of PennCenter - Darrah Hall, dating to 1882,
is the oldest building remaining on the historic campus.

45
Cedar Island National Wildlife Preserve

Carteret County, North Carolina

At land's end 40 miles northeast of Beaufort; take US 70 to NC 12 onto Cedar Island and make a right on Lola Road to headquarters at the end of the road

The Refuge protects almost 15,000 acres - more than 11,000 in brackish marsh - at the confluence of the Pamlico and Core sounds. The coastal marsh is considered the largest on the Atlantic coast.

Only hardcore hikers need apply here. Trails are primitive at best. You can penetrate the heart of the Refuge on a firebreak leading away from the park office. Your best bet is a dirt road off Route 12 in the northwest portion of the Refuge that leads out to Bear Hammock. Expect near-impassable conditions at nearly any time. And in the summer, insect repellent is mandatory - locals are apt to refer to "skeeter island" when mentioning their home on Cedar Island.

46
Palmetto-Peartree Preserve

Tyrell County, North Carolina

Five miles east of Columbia; turn north on SR-1229, left on SR-1221, left on SR-1209, right onto the loop road (SR-1220) and a right in the middle of the loop

It was funding from the North Carolina Department of Transportation that set up the 10,000-acre Palmetto-Peartree Preserve. One of its primary mandates is to shepherd the continued existence of the red-cockaded woodpecker in the face of ongoing road construction in the state. Listed as endangered in 1970, the red-cockaded woodpecker population has declined by 99% since European settlement due to habitat loss and degradation. The male woodpecker has a small red spot behind his eye called a "cockade."

This is a slice of birding heaven on the Albemarle Sound. Separate boardwalk trails visit some sleepy woodlands and the shoreline. More vigorous canine hiking can take place on unpaved Preserve roads, one of which leads to a hidden lake. There is also a canoe launch and paddling trail to take your dog out into the Sound.

47
Abbey Nature Walk at Poplar Grove

New Hanover County, North Carolina
On US 17, approximately nine miles north of Wilmington at Scotts Hill

George Washington was President when James Foy, Jr. purchased 628 acres of land on Topsail Sound from Frances Clayton. When Richard Nixon was leaving office 37 Presidents later the land was still in the Foy family. The current Manor House was built in 1850 and became a museum in 1980. Poplar Grove is one of the oldest existing peanut plantations in North Carolina.

The Foy family placed 67 acres of undeveloped Poplar Grove land into the Coastal Land Trust, reserved for hiking and birding. Dogs are welcome (admission charged) to trot the wide sandy roads of the *Hayride Trail* through dry land forest. Deeper into the Nature Walk it delves into the habitats around wetlands and bottomland forests.

48
Island Creek Forest Walk

Pamlico County, North Carolina
From New Bern go south on US 70 and turn by Trent East Crossing Shopping Center; go to the stop sign and take a left onto SR 1004 and continue 7.5 miles to the trailhead on the right

Deep in the heart of the Croatan National Forest is a stand of old growth hardwood trees that is indeed a rarity on the Carolina coasts. This scenic area around Island Creek was made available to the public by the Trent Woods Garden Club in 1967.

The formal trail is a half-mile interpretive loop, a relaxing hike with your dog under the shade of mixed pines and hardwoods. Look for wildflowers in the spring. There are also unmarked, but well-defined, additional trails that can add an hour to your unhurried stay with your dog here.

49
Patriot's Point Trail

Charleston County, South Carolina

In Mount Pleasant on Patriot's Point Boulevard, south of West Coleman Boulevard (US 17) just over the bridge

Patriot's Point is best known as the home for four museum ships: the *USS Yorktown* (CV-10), an aircraft carrier; *USCGC Ingham* (WHEC-35), a Coast Guard cutter; *USS Laffey* (DD-724), a destroyer; and *USS Clamagore* (SS-343), a submarine. The star is the *USS Yorktown*, one of America's oldest floating aircraft carriers. She earned 11 battle stars and the Presidential Unit Citation during World War II and five battle stars for Vietnam service.

If you are visiting Patriot's Point, this linear trail is a good place to let the dog out for a quick hike. The curvy path runs through a narrow strip of woods that have been left standing between a golf course and athletic fields. Although ten feet on either side of the trail is open space, this place does pull off the illusion of a full woods walk. The *Patriot's Point Trail* ends after almost a mile at an observation tower overlooking a marsh. Although your dog's early steps are on a stony surface it soon improves under paw.

"Dogs' lives are too short. Their only fault, really."
- Agnes Sligh Turnbull

50
Oakhurst Nature Park

Onslow County, North Carolina

In Jacksonville, at the end of Riverbend Road from Ridge Road off Route 258

After their property became part of Camp Lejeune, the Hurst family migrated west, settling on the Blue Creek. Adrian Hurst was the steward of this land keeping it in a natural state - so diligently that it has been designated a "heritage site" as a forest preserved in a pristine state. Hurst died in 1992 and the family sold the land to the North Carolina Coastal Land Trust, who donated it to Onslow County.

The 250 acres on Blue Creek features two nature trails. The longest, at the end of Willbarry Street (as you follow the small brown arrows pointing to the park on Riverbend, stay straight on Willbarry for a few hundred feet), moves on a wide, hard-packed path through a thick pine forest. Many of the trees are under ten feet high so this .7-mile trail has the feel of an English maze garden.

The nature trail at the main parking lot is only half as long but is on natural sandy dirt surfaces. There are also more rolls and dips to the little hike. Here you will find access to Blue Creek for your dog to swim or to launch a canoe and paddle out to the New River.

It is a roomy hike for your dog on the Long Nature Trail through the pines of the Oakhurst Nature park.

Camping With Your Dog On The Carolina Coasts...

North Carolina

Arrowhead Campground
Atlantic Beach
On Route 58, Salter Path Road, south of town.
open April 1 to November 30   (252) 247-3838

Beachcomber Campground
Ocracoke
On Route 12 in town.
open year round   (252) 928-4031

Cabin Creek Campground
Jacksonville
On Route 17, three miles south of the New River Air Station.
open May 1 to November 1   (910) 346-4808

Camp Hatteras
Rodanthe
On Hatteras Island on Route 12.
open year round   (252) 987-2777

Cape Hatteras KOA
Rodanthe
On Hatteras Island on Route 12, 25 miles south of Nags Head.
open year round   (252) 987-2777

Cape Hatteras National Seashore Campgrounds
Manteo
Along Route 12 on Bodie, Hatteras and Ocracoke islands.
Cape Point - Memorial Day to Labor Day
Frisco Campground - Easter to Columbus Day
Ocracoke - Easter to Columbus Day
Oregon Inlet - Easter to Columbus Day   (252) 473-2111

Cape Woods Campground
Buxton
East of Route 12, 1.5 miles south of the Cape Hatteras Lighthouse, off Buxton Village Back Road (Route 1232).
open year round   (252) 987-2777

Carolina Beach State Park
Carolina Beach
On Dow Road, off US 421 ten miles south of Wilmington.
open year-round **(910) 458-8206**

Cedar Creek Campground and Marina
Sea Level
111 Canal Drive off Cedar Creek Road east of Route 70.
open April 1 to November 30 **(252) 225-9571**

Croatan National Forest
Cedar Point Campground
Off Route 58, one mile north of the junction with Route 24.
open year-round **(252) 638-5628**

Croatan National Forest
Neuse River/Flanners Beach Campground
On County Road 1107, north of Route 70.
open year-round **(252) 638-5628**

Croatan National Forest
White Oak River Campground
7600 New Bern Highway (Route 17), one mile south of Route 58.
open year-round **(252) 638-5628**

Cypress Cove Campground
Manteo
At 818 Highway 64 Business, east of US 64/264.
open year-round   **(252) 473-5231**

Driftwood Campground
Cedar Island
At 3575 Cedar Island Road , Route 12, at ferry terminal.
open year round   **(252) 225-4861**

Frisco Woods Campground
Frisco
On Hatteras Island on Route 12 between Buxton and Hatteras Village.
open March 1 to mid-December   **(252) 995-5208**

Goose Creek Resort Family Campground
Newport
At 350 Red Barn Road, 4 miles east on Route 24 from junction with Route 58.
open year round   **(252) 987-2556**

Goose Creek State Park
Washington
On Camp Leach Road off Route 264, ten miles east of town.
open year-round   **(252) 923-2191**

Green Acres Campground
Williamston
Five miles south of town on Route 17 and turn west on Rodgers School Road.
open year-round   **(252) 792-3939**

Hammocks Beach State Park
Swansboro
From Route 24 to Hammocks Beach Road in town to ferry.
open year round   **(910) 326-4881**

Hampton Lodge Camping Resort
Coinjock
At south end of Joseph Palmer Knapp Bridge, 7.2 miles from Route 158 on Waterlily Road.
open year round (877) 832-8333

Hatteras Sands Resort
Frisco
On Hatteras Island on Route 12.
open March 1 to November 30 (252) 986-2422

Holiday Trav-L-Park Resort For Campers
Emerald Isle
9102 Coast Guard Road off Route 58.
open early March to early December (252) 354-2250

Merchants Millpond State Park
Gatesville
On Route 158, north of Route 37.
open year round (252) 357-1191

New Bern KOA
New Bern
On Route 17 north of town.
open year-round   **(252) 638-2556**

Ocean Waves Campground
Waves
On Hatteras Island on Route 12 , 14 miles south of Oregon Inlet.
open March 15 to November 15   **(252) 987-2556**

Pettigrew State Park
Creswell
On Route 64, seven miles south of town.
open year-round   **(252) 797-4475**

Riverside Campground
Belhaven
In town past East Main Street, east of Route 264.
open year-round   **(252) 943-2926**

Rodanthe Watersports and Campground
Rodanthe
On Hatteras Island on Route 12.
open year round   **(252) 987-1431**

S 7 WRV Park
Shallotte
On Holden Beach Road east of Route 17B.
open year-round   **(910) 754-8576**

Salter Path Family Camp Ground
Atlantic Beach
1620 Salter Path Road, Route 58.
open year round   **(252) 247-3525**

Waters Edge RV Park
Newport
On Route 24 between Cape Carteret and Morehead City.
open year-round   **(252) 247-0494**

Waterway Family Campground

Shallotte
4641 Devane Road off Brick Landing Road and Route 179.
open April1 to November 30   (910) 754-8652

Whispering Pines RV Park & Campground

Newport
On Route 24 between Cape Carteret and Morehead City.
open year-round   (252) 726-4902

Wilmington KOA

Wilmington
7415 Market Street, seven miles north of town on Route 17.
open year-round   (910) 686-7705

Apache Oceanfront Family Campground
Myrtle Beach
On Kings Road, 1.5 miles east of Route 17.
open year-round   **(843) 449-7323**

Barefoot Camping Resort
North Myrtle Beach
At 4825 Route 17 South, north of Veterans Highway.
open year round   **(843) 272-1790**

Charleston KOA
Ladson
On Route 78, one mile west of I-26.
open year-round   **(843) 797-1045**

Edisto Beach State Park
Edisto Island
On Route 174 at 8377 State Cabin Road.
open year round   **(843) 869-2756**

Francis Marion National Forest
Buck Hall Recreation Area
Six miles southeast of McClellanville on Buck Hall Landing Road off Route 17.
open year round   **(843) 887-3257**

Givhans Ferry State Park
Ridgeville
At 746 Givhans Ferry Road off Route 61, 16 miles west of Charleston.
open year-round   **(843) 873-0692**

Hilton Head Harbor RV Resort & Marina
Hilton Head Island
At 43A Jenkins Road off Route 278, one mile southeast of the Intracoastal Waterway Beach.
open year round   **(843) 681-3256**

Hunting Island State Park
Beaufort
On Route 21, 16 miles east of town.
open year-round (843) 838-2011

Huntington Beach State Park
Murrells Inlet
At 16148 Ocean Highway (Route 17).
open year round (843) 237-4440

James Island County Park
Charleston
From Route 17 to Route 171 south to the Maybank Highway (Route 700); go west and turn onto Riverland Drive.
open year-round (843) 795-4386

Lakewood Camping Resort
Myrtle Beach
At 5901 South Kings Highway (Route 17 Business), a half-mile north of junction with Route 544.
open year round (843) 238-5161

Mount Pleasant/Charleston KOA Campground
Mount Pleasant
On Route 174 at 8377 State Cabin Road.
open year round (843) 849-5177

Myrtle Beach KOA
Myrtle Beach
At 613 5th Avenue South off Route 17 Business, south of Highway 501.
open year-round (843) 448-3421

Myrtle Beach RV Resort
North Myrtle Beach
At 5400 Little River Neck Road, three miles northeast of Route 17 at the Cherry Grove exit.
open year round (843) 249-1484

Myrtle Beach State Park

Myrtle Beach
On South Kings Highway (Route 17) south of town.
open year-round   **(843) 238-5325**

Myrtle Beach Travel Park

Myrtle Beach
10108 Kings Road, off Route 17 Business, north of Highway 501.
open year round   **(843) 449-3174**

Ocean Lakes Family Campground

Myrtle Beach
6001 South Kings Highway (Route 17 Business) at junction of Route 544.
open year-round   **(843) 238-5636**

Pirateland Family Camping Resort

Myrtle Beach
At 5401 South Kings Highway (Route 17 Business), north of junction with Route 544.
open year round   **(843) 238-5155**

Stoney Crest Plantation Campground

Bluffton
On Route 46, seven miles west of Route 278 Business.
open year round   **(843) 757-3249**

Your Dog On The Carolina Coast Beaches...

It is hard to imagine many places a dog is happier than at a beach. Whether running around on the sand, jumping in the water or just lying in the sun, every dog deserves a day at the beach. But all too often dog owners stopping at a sandy stretch of beach are met with signs designed to make hearts - human and canine alike - droop: NO DOGS ON BEACH. Below are rules for taking your dog on a day trip to an Atlantic Ocean beach on the Carolina coasts (*from north to south*).

North Carolina

OUTER BANKS

Corolla	**Dogs allowed on beach under voice control**
Duck	**Unleashed dogs allowed on beach**
Kill Devil Hills	**Dogs allowed on the beach from mid-September to mid-May**
Kitty Hawk	**Dogs are allowed unleashed on the beach September 1 to June 1 and before 10 a.m. and after 6 p.m. otherwise; leashed dogs allowed on beach 10 a.m. to 6 p.m. June 1 to September 1**
Nags Head	**Dogs allowed on beach year-round on a 10-foot leash**
Southern Shores	**Leashed dogs allowed on beach September 15 to May 15**
Cape Hatteras National Seashore	**Dogs allowed on beach year-round on a 6-foot leash**
Ocracoke Island	**Dogs allowed on beach year-round on a 6-foot leash**

Cape Lookout National Seashore	Dogs allowed on beach year-round on a 6-foot leash
Atlantic Beach – Fort Macon	Dogs allowed on the non-swimming beach
Atlantic Beach – Town Beach	Leashed dogs allowed on beach except in the Circle and the beach area in front of the Circle from Easter to Labor Day
Pine Knolls	Dogs allowed anytime on beach with a 16-foot maximum leash
Salter Path	Dogs allowed on leash anytime
Indian Beach	No posted beach restrictions for dogs
Emerald Isle	Leashed dogs allowed on beach anytime
Hammocks Beach State Park	Leashed dogs are allowed on any beach that is not a swimming beach

CAPE FEAR

Topsail Beach	Leashed dogs allowed May 15 through September 30 and under voice control at other times
Wrightsville Beach	Leashed dogs allowed on beach from October 1 to April 1
Carolna Beach	No dogs allowed on beach March 1 to October 31
Kure Beach	No dogs allowed on beach April to September
Fort Fisher State Recreation Area	Leashed dogs allowed on beach in any non-swimming area

Caswell Beach	**Leashed dogs allowed on beach**
Oak Island	**Leashed dogs allowed on beach**
Holden Beach	**Leashed dogs allowed on beach Labor Day to Memorial Day and during the summer before 9 a.m. and after 5 p.m.**
Ocean Isle Beach	**Leashed dogs allowed on beach Labor Day to Memorial Day and during the summer before 9 a.m. and after 6 p.m.**
Sunset Beach	**Leashed dogs allowed on beach Labor Day to Memorial Day and during the summer before 8 a.m. and after 6 p.m.**
Indian Beach	**No posted beach restrictions for dogs**
Emerald Isle	**Leashed dogs allowed on beach anytime**
Hammocks Beach State Park	**Leashed dogs are allowed on any beach that is not a swimming beach**

South Carolina

North Myrtle Beach	**Dogs allowed on the beach September 15 to May 15 anytime and before 9 a.m. and after 5 p.m. otherwise**
Myrtle Beach	**No dogs ever allowed on the beach from 21st Avenue North to 13th Avenue South; otherwise dogs allowed on the beach September 15 to May 15 anytime and before 9:00 a.m and after 5:00 p.m. in the summer**
Surfside Beach	**Dogs allowed on beach September 16 to May 14**
Garden City Beach	**Dogs allowed on beach under voice control**

Myrtle Beach – Myrtle Beach State Park	Leashed dogs allowed on the beach year-round
Murrells Inlet – Huntington State Park	Leashed dogs allowed on the beach year-round
Litchfield Beach	Dogs allowed on beach under voice control
Pawleys Island	Leashed dogs allowed on beach May to October; under voice control other times
Georgetown	Leashed dogs allowed on beach
Isle of Palms	Dogs allowed on beach under voice control from 5 a.m. to 8 a.m. with owner holding leash; leashed dogs allowed on beach other times
Sullivans Island	No dogs 10 a.m. to 6 p.m April 1 to October 31; allowed off-leash before 10 a.m. and on leash after 6:00 p.m., from November 1 to March 31 dogs are allowed off-leash from 5:00 a.m. to noon
Folly Beach	Dogs allowed on the beach in the evenings in summer and the entire day the rest of the year
Kiawah Island – Beachwalker Park	Leashed dogs allowed from March 15 to October 31 and under voice control the rest of the year
Edisto Beach	Leashed dogs allowed on beach anytime
Beaufort – Hunting Island State Park	Leashed dogs allowed on the beach year-round
Hilton Head Island – Driessden's Beach	Leashed dogs are allowed on beach
Hilton Head Island – Folly Field Beach	Leashed dogs are allowed on beach

Tips For Taking Your Dog To The Beach

- The majority of dogs can swim and love it, but dogs entering the water for the first time should be tested; never throw a dog into the water. Start in shallow water and call your dog's name - or try to coax him in with a treat or toy. Always keep your dog within reach.

- Another way to introduce your dog to the water is with a dog that already swims and is friendly with your dog. Let your dog follow his friend.

- If your dog begins to doggie paddle with his front legs only, lift his hind legs and help him float. He should quickly catch on and will keep his back end up.

- Swimming is a great form of exercise, but don't let your dog overdo it. He will be using new muscles and may tire quickly.

- Be careful of strong tides that are hazardous for even the best swimmers.

- Cool ocean water is tempting to your dog. Do not allow him to drink too much sea water. Salt in the water will make him sick. Salt and other minerals found in the ocean can damage your dog's coat so regular bathing is essential.

- Check with a lifeguard for daily water conditions - dogs are easy targets for jellyfish and sea lice.

- Dogs can get sunburned, especially short-haired dogs and ones with pink skin and white hair. Limit your dog's exposure when the sun is strong and apply sunblock to his ears and nose 30 minutes before going outside.

- If your dog is out of shape, don't encourage him to run on the sand, which is strenuous exercise and a dog that is out of shape can easily pull a tendon or ligament.

Index To Parks and Open Spaces

North Carolina   *page*

Abbey Nature Walk at Poplar Grove	104
Alligator River National Wildlife Refuge	82
Bird Island Coastal Reserve	80
Cape Hatteras National Seashore	22
Carolina Beach State Park	36
Cedar Island National Wildlife Refuge	103
Cedar Point Recreation Area	62
Currituck Heritage Park	84
Currituck National Wildlife Refuge	66
Dismal Swamp Canal Trail	92
Emerald Isle Woods Park	96
Flanners Beach Trail	100
Fort Fisher State Recreation Area	32
Fort Macon State Park	52
Fort Raleigh National Historic Area	70
Goose Creek State Park	28
Hugh MacRae Park	86
Island Creek Forest Walk	104
Jockey's Ridge State Park	26
Mackay Island National Wildlife Refuge	76
Merchants Millpond State Park	50
Moores Creek National Battlefield	78
Neusiok Trail	58
Oakhurst Nature Park	106
Palmetto-Peartree Preserve	103
Patsy Pond Nature Trail	44
Pettigrew State Park	48
Pocosin Lakes National Wildlife Refuge	94
Wright Brothers National Memorial	88

South Carolina   *page*

ACE Basin National Wildlife Refuge	60
Audubon Newhall Preserve	54
Awendaw Passage/Palmetto Trail	56
Charles Pinckney National Historic Site	101
Dungannon Plantation Heritage Preserve	48
Edisto Beach State Park	30
Edisto Nature Trail	46
Fort Lamar Heritage Preserve	100
Fort Moultrie	72
Hunting Island State Park	20
Huntington Beach State Park	24
James Island County Park	90
Magnolia Plantation & Gardens	34
Mt. Pleasant Palmetto Islands County Park	40
Myrtle Beach State Park	38
Patriot's Point Trail	105
Penn Nature Center	102
Santee Coastal Reserve	64
South Tibwin Hiking Trail	68
Wannamaker County Park	74
West Ashley Greenway	98